StoryMaking

StoryMaking

The Maker Movement Approach
to Literacy for Early Learners

Michelle Kay Compton, MA

Robin Chappele Thompson, PhD

Redleaf Press®
www.redleafpress.org
800-423-8309

Published by Redleaf Press
10 Yorkton Court
St. Paul, MN 55117
www.redleafpress.org

First edition 2018
Cover design by Tom Heffron
Cover photo by Kikovic, Getty Images / iStockphoto
Interior design by Percolator
Typeset in Elena
Printed in the United States of America
25 24 23 22 21 20 19 18   1 2 3 4 5 6 7 8

Library of Congress Cataloging-in-Publication Data

Names: Compton, Michelle Kay, author. | Thompson, Robin, 1960– author.
Title: Storymaking : the maker movement approach to literacy for early learners / Michelle Kay
    Compton, Robin Chappele Thompson.
Description: St. Paul, MN : Redleaf Press, 2018. | Includes bibliographical references and index.
Identifiers: LCCN 2018002004 (print) | LCCN 2018017107 (ebook) | ISBN 9781605546049 (ebook)
    | ISBN 9781605546032 (pbk. : alk. paper)
Subjects: LCSH: Reading (Early childhood) | Storytelling in education. | Maker movement in
    education. | Reggio Emilia approach (Early childhood education)
Classification: LCC LB1139.5.R43 (ebook) | LCC LB1139.5.R43 C65 2018 (print) | DDC 372.4—dc23
LC record available at https://lccn.loc.gov/2018002004

Printed on acid-free paper

For Shawn,

    who creates a life with me full of stories worth sharing,

and for Cole and Cai,

    who will inspire the world with their imaginations.

—MKC

For my parents,

    who gave me the guidance and freedom to imagine my stories,

and for Wade,

    who makes my stories even better than I imagined.

—RCT

Contents

Foreword

This winter, I was sitting at my kitchen counter with a fresh cup of coffee, outlining a new concept for a block-building platform that the company I founded, Kodo Kids, was designing for preschool classrooms. My twin seven-year-old daughters sat by the fire in the living room chattering away, playing with clay creatures they had created earlier in the day. I found my focus drifting to their conversation. They were engrossed in a story, set in a forest with many different creatures and an ever changing plot line and setting. Their story flowed smoothly, evolving and weaving as the characters bounced from terrifying situations to hilarious laughter. The clay characters changed along with the story, my daughters continually remolding them as they moved the story in yet another direction.

Maybe it caught my attention because a few months earlier, at the NAEYC conference in 2017, I met Michelle and Robin, the authors of this book. After attending my Maker presentation, they visited the Kodo Kids booth in the exhibit hall. Within thirty seconds we all could feel the synergy between Kodo's products and their approach with StoryMaking in the classroom. We were speaking the same language and saw the natural potential to support each other's efforts.

That morning back at home as my attention went back and forth between my daughters' story and my design project, I realized we were involved in the same process: the methodology they were using to make their story was the same as my design process. At Kodo, we approach our designs as open-ended workspaces that kids can adapt to meet their needs during play. My daughters' play that day was the same kind of open-ended workspace that they adapted to support their ever-changing storyline. As I went back to my work, I was reminded how our designs support this type of play and had a new understanding of what directs our design process.

At Kodo, innovation comes from play, experimentation, and a creative mindset. That morning I realized that as ideas unfold they are placed into a contextual story between the child, the materials, the classroom, and the teacher. To develop the product concept we explore a multitude of storylines, changing the plot and characters to envision the many possibilities the product provides for the classroom. The concept develops and if it makes the cut, yields the best, most impactful products for children, their teachers, and the classroom. As an entrepreneur, this empathetic approach to understanding the customer through story is not only at the heart of impactful products but also a successful business.

In this book, Michelle and Robin have thoughtfully outlined an approach and purpose to foster this kind of engaged design and entrepreneurial thinking, providing a foundation for children's future learning. Combining the concept of story with the new educational trend of Makerspaces, *StoryMaking* is an impactful read that is sure to have direct implications on your teaching practice. Most importantly it will benefit the many children who will be exposed the StoryMaking experience.

In the past few years, Kodo has been watching the Maker Movement begin to gain traction in early education just as it has in K–12. But teachers, curriculum coordinators, and directors are still looking for meaningful ways to implement Maker with their children. This book lays out how to put story Makerspaces into action in the classroom. The authors give many examples and the results of their intentions are clear, with great imagery and real life situations from the classroom.

As a Maker myself, I rely on the experiences I had as a young child, exploring, tinkering with loose parts, working through challenges, and generally following a story as I explored the world around me. My action figures in combination with Lego creations set the stage for hours of creative play, which thankfully my parents supported by supplying other materials that I used to build and construct (while miraculously *not* cutting off my fingers). During hours of freeform experimentation I learned to persevere in constructing the settings for my stories to unfold.

Now as an adult, reading this book reminds me of the possibilities that story creation yields in supporting key skills and mindsets like the abilities to conceptualize, brainstorm, create, and collaborate that are essential to success in design. The authors frame these kills as the StoryMaker Cycle of Imagine, Play, Make, and Share. From launching new initiatives, to developing new products, I am continuously building the story around my objectives and adapting that story as priorities quickly change to meet my goals for the day, month, or year. Many people must struggle to develop these skills as adults. The children who are featured in this book and the many who have had the StoryMaking experience, have mastered these skills well ahead of the curve! What a tremendous advantage these children have as they move ahead in life.

The combination of StoryMaking and Makerspaces is incredibly powerful! In StoryMaking, the creation of content is constrained by your imagination and the experiences you have to pull from; in making physical objects or systems, you are constrained by the materials you have at hand and your knowledge base of how things work. Together, these are two manifestation of the same philosophy, leading to an explosion of experiential learning and hands on comprehension interwoven with core literacy development!

StoryMaking supports current trends in Early Education. With the focus on STEAM at all levels of education and the recognized importance of early years play in building technical skills, *StoryMaking* can help to provide the foundation for STEAM learning. Engineers, scientists, and technical professionals use a breadth of knowledge to problem-solve and find solutions to complex problems. Building this base of knowledge, skills, and mindsets starts at birth. As children play and experiment, they are exposed to new materials, methods, and concepts that build that essential knowledge and understanding, strengthening STEAM skills. As makers, children put STEAM concepts to work, making the learning relevant and impactful. These experiences lay the groundwork that supports future learning.

In addition to "hard" skills, the StoryMaking approach supports all those "soft" skills that are so essential—things like problem-solving, perseverance, empathy, and communication skills among many other key life skills. As pointed out in new research by Google, these are the skills that businesses are looking for in their workforce, even above and beyond technical skills. In each area of the StoryMaking Cycle (Imagine, Make, Play, and Share), kids use these soft skills, revisiting them again and again throughout the book. Not only are the children learning STEAM concepts, but they are learning how to use and communicate them in context, with other children and adults, all while actively thinking, planning, and progressing their story.

I am honored to be asked to write this foreword. The work Michelle and Robin have done so nicely matches the mission we are looking to fulfill. As you read, notice how the teachers support children in their learning by upholding their natural tendency of playing, learning, and growing through story. As teachers and leaders in early childhood education, we have the amazing opportunity to help children in their learning by supporting and enriching their experiences in the classroom. I hope you enjoy *StoryMaking* as I have, and can put into practice the many insights you will gain.

—Chris Hume
Founder, Kodo Kids

Acknowledgments

Michelle

I feel blessed to be surrounded by a culture not only of StoryMakers, but also of individuals who have made it their goal to make my dreams come true!

Robin, you truly are a dream maker! Thank you for giving me the freedom to research and tinker with these ideas with our teachers. I am so grateful for your listening ear, collaborative nature, and adventurous spirit. Our journey has just begun!

Teachers, I want to sincerely thank you for trusting me to try out these ideas with your children. You made the dream of StoryMakers come alive. A special thank-you to Rachel Spivey, Tara Legowski, and Shannon Rivard, who first allowed me into their classrooms, developed lessons together, and tolerated me videoing as much as I could to document this wonderful experience. I also want to thank Peggy Welch, Lori Vaughan, Angela Leggett, Katie Choate, and Laurie Funderburk for joining the project and being risk-takers by fully implementing StoryMaking in their classrooms for the entire year. You each brought your own talented ideas to this project, and I am grateful for your collaboration and friendship.

Mom, thank you for being such a strong role model who raised me to believe that if you can dream it, it can come true.

Shawn, you are my ultimate dream maker and the rock of our family. Thank you for always finding a way to make my dreams come true. I am able to make and share such joyful stories because of the life we are making together. I am excited to see what new adventures we create together as we turn to another chapter in our book.

Cole and Cai, this book is for you. This kind of education is what I dream for you—a learning environment where you are free to imagine, play, make, and share your own stories. Thank you for being so patient with Mommy. I hope you know that I will always have time to play and make stories together.

Robin

Michelle, thank you for inviting me to take this journey with you. I have loved every minute. I can't wait to see what comes next!

Teachers, thank you for inviting me into your classrooms to imagine, play, make, and share. You are a most amazing group of women who are smart, strong, and doing the hard work. The good work. Thank you for sharing your expertise, talents, and thoughts. Without you, this project would not have been possible.

Dr. Greene, thank you for trusting us to innovate as we explored, investigated, figured out, and implemented what is best for young children as they learn and grow.

Wade, thank you. You are the protagonist of my story, the most amazing husband, hero, tinkerer, fixer, cook, gardener, friend, parent, carpenter, adventure partner, and on and on. I love making our story together.

Dacie and Glori, you are precious and beloved jewels in my story. You have made my story joyful and full of laughter. And Dennis, you are a treasured addition to our story. This is for my grandchildren-to-be, my great-nieces and nephews-to-be, and Raleigh. I can't wait to add more StoryMakers to our family!

We would both like to thank Redleaf for imagining a space for us in their library. We feel honored to have the opportunity to tell our story and to help inspire other educators to build a StoryMaking culture in their own learning environments. Also, we would like to thank our editor, Andrea Rud, for her countless hours and dedication to help make this the best version of our story to share.

Introduction

Ms. Shannon, a pre-K teacher, was gathered around a group of boys actively playing with blocks and other loose parts. She asked one of the four-year-olds, "What are you making?" Jayden said, "I saw an otter at the zoo." He was re-creating the habitat with his materials to share about his experience at the zoo. A few days later, Jayden was using art materials. Ms. Shannon asked, "What are you making?" Jayden continued talking about the zoo and added that there were tigers. He selected orange and black crayons to make marks on the page and then told his story aloud to her. "One day, there were otters at the zoo. The lions and the tigers were playing with each other." Jayden had learned that what he made and what he drew held meaning—they held his story to share. He then asked if he could take his story to paper and write it to share with the class.

This is the beauty of StoryMaking! It allows the child to use their creativity and materials to make (the maker), orally express a story (the storyteller), explore shapes and techniques to illustrate (the artist), and investigate how marks and letter formations can be made on paper (the writer). In today's early learning environments, there is an increasing amount of pressure to decrease the time for play to make way for academic mandates. StoryMaking allows playing with materials to be at the core of your children's day so they can imagine, play, make, and share the stories of their lives.

OUR DAY JOBS

Michelle and I work in a public school district that has over 48,000 students enrolled in pre-K through twelfth grade. We are honored to work with our district's Early Learning Team and the prekindergarten teachers and children. Our early learning team is full of deep thinkers and researchers who are curious, questioning, and constantly seeking new ways to engage and develop our early learners and their teachers. Our teachers are willing to take risks, try out new ideas, and follow the children in their interests, wonderings, and curiosities. And our children—we are amazed by our students and their brilliant minds, their questions, their innovations, and the lessons they teach us every day. We love what we do!

We currently have over one thousand prekindergarten students enrolled in our early learning programs. We have a diverse student population in our school system, which is 48 percent Caucasian, 14 percent African American, and 33 percent Hispanic. Approximately 55 percent of our students are considered economically disadvantaged. We have twenty Title I schools with about forty classrooms of prekindergarten students, where more than 75 percent of the student population qualifies for free and reduced lunches. Our prekindergarten classrooms include children with special rights (needs), inclusion classrooms, and typically developing students.

We have a diverse set of teachers in our classrooms. Some of our classrooms are taught by teachers with bachelor's degrees, master's degrees, or alternative certification; while other classrooms have a lead teacher who has earned a child development associate credential.

HOW STORYMAKING WAS BORN

In the past, our state assessment had indicated some weaknesses in the oral language skills of our students. Because we were most interested in improving and scaffolding the oral language development of our youngest children, our main purpose for implementing StoryMaking was to address these needs in this particular domain—but we wanted the learning to include play and fun! And we hoped for learning across many disciplines rather than just isolated skill and drill. We wanted to create a structure within which we could meet state expectations for our young learners while still honoring their literacies, their wonderings, and their creativity.

Our district had implemented an initiative to increase student engagement; therefore, we knew whatever we instituted needed to be highly engaging for our youngest learners. We had been investigating possibilities embedded in the maker movement, a trend where students use stuff to make stuff, and learn in the process (Heroman 2017, 4). Through our research, we discovered Opal School's Story Workshop and wondered how we could support children in making stories with a variety of materials witnessed throughout the maker movement? We definitely believed our students were makers, as "makers are curious people, whose interest in and wonder about a particular topic leads to inquiry and exploration" (Brahms and Crowley 2016, 20). We wanted to incorporate learning through making and playing in order to create an interest-driven and inclusive community where we could celebrate our students' innovations, wonderings, histories, and stories. Making is usually focused on STEAM (science, technology, engineering, arts, mathematics) and not oral language. However, "to focus on STEM skills and the like as the primary outcome of maker-centered learning would be to sadly miss the point . . . the power of maker-centered learning is to help students develop a sense of personal agency and self-efficacy" (Ryan et al. 2016, 35).

In accordance with Loris Malaguzzi and the philosophy of Reggio Emilia, we believe all children are intelligent, creative, and resourceful, and they communicate their individual gifts in many different "languages," including visual arts, building blocks, collage, dance, tinkering, music, movement, literacy, math, science, social-emotional languages, and physical languages. We wanted to provide students with opportunities to make their stories using the languages and open-ended materials of their choice. StoryMaking was our way of maintaining compliance to the standards; addressing oral language, an area of weakness; and introducing making, the learning practices, the maker's mind-set, and engagement in the processes of making. Thus, StoryMaking was born.

StoryMaking requires a few things. First, a *maker*. A maker is "someone—anyone—who makes things" (Clapp et al. 2017, 5). Our young children are the makers in StoryMaking. Second, a space for making. A *Makerspace* is a "place where people gather to tinker, make things, invent, create, explore, and make discoveries using a wide variety of real tools" (Heroman 2017, 5). Next, a story. Children come to us with stories that result from their unique family, history, experiences, perspective, and wonderings. Also, we need materials. Our makers use stuff (tools, artifacts, items, loose parts) to make their stories. Finally, a process is required to take all the aforementioned elements and make the story. We watched children making their stories, took notes, and analyzed and categorized what they did. They used their imaginations, played, made, and shared. That's our StoryMaker Cycle. Our young learners imagine, play, make, and share the everyday stories of their lives. They StoryMake.

We hope to inspire you to create your own version of StoryMaking, one that meets the needs of you and your children. We can't wait for you to join us on this journey. We will try to warn you about mistakes we made so you can avoid them. And we look forward to hearing from you about your innovations and ideas. Let's get started!

HOW THIS BOOK IS ORGANIZED

We've developed the chapters in chronological order for implementing Story-Making. If you start at the beginning, then you'll be able to implement and try things out as you read and then read some more to try out next steps. Or feel free to skip around to meet your needs. You may not need information on materials, for example, so you could skip that part of chapter 2.

Chapter 1 discusses what StoryMaking is and shows what it looks like in a space with young children. We will introduce our StoryMaker Cycle and detail its components, including the learning practices of the maker's movement enacted during StoryMaking. Chapter 2 helps you prepare to get started with StoryMaking by focusing on the classroom environment. We will discuss how to find time in your day for StoryMaking, how to use your areas for StoryMaking, and what materials you may select to prepare for making stories. Chapter 3 provides a rationale and how-to guide for building a culture of StoryMaking in your classroom, details how to set up a framework for inquiry in preparation for your culture of StoryMaking, describes the inquiry cycle we use in our classrooms, and provides examples of behaviors we've observed during StoryMaking. Chapter 4 offers practical suggestions for how to get started with StoryMaking. We propose lessons and present scripts for launching Phase 1 of StoryMaking. Chapter 5 helps you move successfully into Phase 2 and includes lesson plans and practical suggestions for re-engaging the learner, changing the environment, offering new provocations, and using mentor texts. Chapter 6 outlines lessons for Phase 3 and includes examples of the numerous languages used to represent stories in our classrooms and a variety of possibilities for sharing the students' stories. Chapter 7 explores documentation and assessment and includes documents that make it easy to keep track of every story and the progress of your students.

There are also some common features that you can look forward to throughout the book. In the beginning of each chapter, we highlight a classroom example of what StoryMaking looks like. Teachers don't want to be lectured on how to do something. They may not have time to read pages and pages of research. They just want to see what it looks like. Although new initiatives can bring some angst ("Not another thing we have to do."), we have found that after seeing what something looks like, our teachers say, "I can do that" or "I already do most of that. I just have to change one little thing." So that's how we will start. We include a narrative, accompanied by photographs of students, their work, their words, and other forms of documentation.

We also share the experiences of those who have implemented StoryMaking, in their own words. Our teachers took risks, shared honestly, and grew in their pedagogical practices. They will discuss mistakes made, lessons learned, and improvements made along the way. You need to hear from them.

Special Rights. Each chapter includes accommodations and invitations for students with diverse needs, including those with special needs and English-language learners. We refer to children who have been identified with special needs as children with *special rights*, in accordance with the philosophy of Reggio Emilia. This is not to say they have *more* rights than other children but that their rights may have to be coordinated by the school, the medical community, social service providers, and other outside agencies, and not everyone is always aware of children's rights. Children with special rights might require special attention, customized materials, or diverse opportunities for learning. One of the things we love about StoryMaking is its inclusivity. It offers all students access points to learning. It provides opportunities for them to share their literacies using languages that are accessible to them (such as dance, drawing, clay, sculpture). StoryMaking honors multimodal representations of literacies and provides opportunities for teachers to monitor progress and document learning for all students. Given the diverse learners in our classrooms, we must develop ways to grow our students' literacies, document this growth, and be able to identify next steps. StoryMaking makes this possible.

Maker's Moment. Documenting the stories and successes along the way is extremely important to moving StoryMaking forward. Therefore, we take a break at the end of each chapter to pause and reflect on what was learned with a documentation story. It provides an opportunity to look inside the classrooms we worked in and meet the StoryMakers who made so many powerful stories that they were proud to share. We hope you take this time not only to revisit what you learned in the chapter but also to celebrate the accomplishments of each StoryMaker!

We are now ready to share all of our ideas, research, and resources with you. We've tried to present a research-based rationale for our decisions in order to form a foundation from which you can make your own good decisions. We won't present the research and then leave you on your own to figure out how to translate it to practical application with young learners. We'll provide you with all sorts of practical applications and the supporting documentation that will guide your thinking and decision-making processes.

Through this book, we have created a culture of StoryMaking for grown-ups where you are welcomed, invited to participate, and encouraged to hack and repurpose what we show you to meet the needs of your situation and children. We are an inclusive community, all learning and growing together. Each of us has our own areas of expertise and each of us has a story, perhaps ready to be re-imagined, played with and reconfigured, made anew, and shared. We invite you to become part of our culture for StoryMaking. Please join us!

CHAPTER 1

What Is StoryMaking?

A CLASSROOM BUZZING WITH STORIES

I walked into Ms. Shannon's classroom just in time for the focus lesson to begin. A focus lesson is a short lesson that has a purpose for learning, where teachers model, demonstrate, or share their thinking. All the children were gathered on the carpet. Michelle was teaching the lesson while Ms. Shannon observed and videotaped. Michelle started out with "Good morning, StoryMakers!" The children smiled and bounced up and down on their knees. They have come to include "StoryMaker" as a part of their identity; after all, they make stories every day! Michelle and Ms. Shannon have been using mentor texts to explicitly teach visual literacy skills to the children during StoryMaking. Mentor texts are pieces of literature that you—both teacher and student—can return to and reread for many different purposes (see more on mentor texts on page 82). The children were examining the illustrations in the mentor texts; discussing how emotions, context, and details are conveyed in illustrations; and then trying to replicate and apply the lessons learned to their own stories.

MICHELLE: What is the feeling in this picture?
ANNABEL: Silly.
MICHELLE: Why?
ANNABEL: She's acting silly.
MICHELLE: Describe what silly looks like.
ANNABEL: She's doing this with her mouth. (Makes a face.) Playing with her
    hands. The eyebrows is up here and making silly.

Michelle turns back to a picture in the mentor text that was discussed yesterday. It depicts a scared character.

MICHELLE: Show me *scared*.
    (Annabel and the other children make scared faces.)

MICHELLE: What can I learn from the illustrator to include in my picture?
ANNABEL: Her hair is going up to show she is scared.
CALI: The eyeballs looked big. The hair is straight up.

Michelle wrote *facial expressions* on a sticky note and placed it next to the character's face in the story illustration to annotate the image with vocabulary and make the strategy clear for the students.

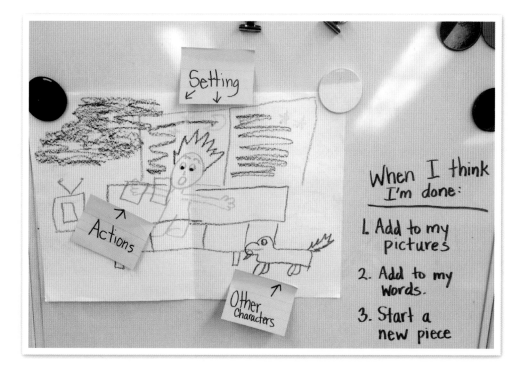

Annotated illustration teaches children how to add details to their drawings.

The students were all engaged in the conversation, making faces, acting out what it looks like to be silly and scared. After a short conversation and a few more examples from the mentor text, the students were given some "think time." They turned and talked to their partners about their stories and discussed how they were going to add details and colors to their illustrations to convey the emotions of their characters. One of the children turned to talk to me about her story:

DALLASHIA: My story is about when I was in the bed sleeping. Gwendolyn
    scared me and said, "Peekaboo."

After sharing some highlights from the students' story ideas, it is time for each of the children to imagine what materials might best convey the stories they are making.

LAILAH: My story is about me and my mom. I scared her.
MICHELLE: What material are you going to use to make your story?

LAILAH: Collage.

MICHELLE: Off you go.

(*Lailah moves quickly to the collage table and starts making her story.*)

Lailah makes her story with collage materials.

The children were all excited to play, as they continued stories they'd been working on or started new stories. Within two minutes the classroom was buzzing with stories. Students were engaged in exploring, making, and growing their stories. Some students were StoryMaking together while others worked quietly by themselves. Ms. Shannon had a document on a clipboard that she used daily to remind herself where each child was in the process of StoryMaking (see "Recording," pages 133–36, for information on documentation forms). She checked in with the children, visiting and conferring with them in their Makerspaces as they played.

Ms. Shannon uses documentation forms to record stories.

I first visited the attachments area. There were sticks, twigs, tape, glue, rubber bands, cardboard, clothespins, clips, and so on. We believe all spaces in the classroom can become Makerspaces, and this Makerspace came to be called "attachments," as the children used the space to figure out how to use tools and materials to connect objects in order to make the people, places, and things in their stories. And connect they did! As Gabriel left the circle, I heard him tell another classmate, "I'm going to make something." He headed straight for the attachments Makerspace. I later talked to Ms. Shannon about Gabriel and his work in that space. She said, "I remember his story clearly because this was the first real connection he made in school." The initial purpose of the space was for the children to gain fluency using tools, but they used it for a variety of purposes as they played and made their stories there.

I went next to the drawing table, where four girls were working, talking, and adding details to their stories. There were crayons, oil pastels, thin and thick markers, chalk, and an ample supply of blank white paper. The girls were narrating their stories as they were drawing, answering one another's questions about their color choices, emotions, materials selections, and story plots. A boy joined the group and there was some negotiation with regard to sharing ("I'm using the crayons."); friendship ("Are you being my friend?"); and manners ("Don't call him that."). In less than a minute they were all back at work, exploring the materials, posing and answering one another's questions, seeking one another's opinions, playing, and making their stories, with the boy accepted as part of the community.

Children use art materials to begin making their stories.

As Dallashia was drawing, she started telling me her story. It had grown in just the few minutes since she had shared it with me during the focus lesson. She had hacked and repurposed it so that it now included a ghost, some dialogue, and details about its setting and emotions.

> Gwendolyn scared me when I was sleeping. And there was a ghost. That's me and Gwendolyn. (*She points to her drawing.*) The real ghost is right here. And Gwendolyn is right here. She said, "We are going to go to sleep." And she scaring me. Mommy was in the living room. And Gwendolyn told me to stay in the bed. That's me. I look scared. Mommy said, "Let me out." To Gwendolyn. The door is closed.

I wanted a chance to visit other stories, so I reluctantly left the drawing table. I passed the area filled with Legos on my way to collage. Three boys and two girls were making their stories. There was a castle being built out of Legos. A Batman made of Legos was flying. Each child was concentrating on creating settings, characters, and details as they played, made, and grew their stories. Materials were customized by the children to fit their stories as they were being made.

In another Makerspace was a plethora of collage materials. Open plastic tackle boxes were full of treasures. The compartments contained colorful parts and pieces—recycled materials, loose parts, crafting supplies. All were inviting. One box had pom-poms, feathers, buttons, wooden discs, glass beads, wooden craft sticks, wooden spoons, and more. There were rubber sheets, felt pieces, colored paper, mentor texts, construction paper, and glue.

Two girls were making their stories in collage. They both started with blank canvases. One selected a light-blue felt, while the other chose navy construction paper, "like night." They were talking to each other about which materials would make the best people and what hairstyles their characters should have: they were relying on each other as resources with expertise. They passed a long, braided piece of yarn back and forth between them, trying it on their characters. They finally chose which character it looked best on. She was a wooden spoon with a long braid. They discussed that there could be blood when they removed her braid and how the blood would be scary. I heard them use the words *scary* and *silly* during the course of their conversation—words that had been introduced during the focus lesson of the illustration study. When I asked, neither was ready to share her story. Then one of the girls changed her mind and decided to share a bit:

> My story is about my mom was reading a book. And then I made a scary noise and my mom was scary. Then my fish looked up. Like this. (*She makes a scary face.*)

I moved to a block Makerspace. This area had gigantic wooden blocks, stained, with the grains of the wood showing through. There were two students, a girl and a boy. The boy had three cars balanced on top of a tower of blocks. The cars were arranged by size: small next to medium next to large. He also had a small car on his knee that he was moving back and forth along his leg. The girl had a menagerie of small plastic creatures next to her and a dolphin in her hand that was swimming toward the three cars on the tower. The two children were dialoguing back and forth, moving the dolphin and the car. I couldn't hear all of what they were saying, but they were constructing a story together, each using different materials.

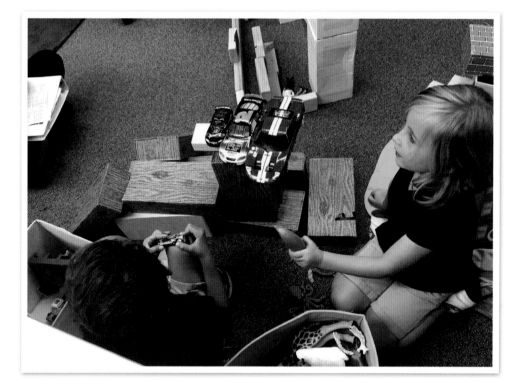

Children are playing and making their stories in the block Makerspace.

In another area, two boys had constructed a wooden bridge connecting two tall towers of shoeboxes. The boys were intently engaged in making their story together.

I moved to the housekeeping Makerspace, which had been converted to a quiet space for writing. A girl was working by herself. She had drawn a detailed picture to which she was adding sticky notes, as Michelle had done during the focus lesson. She was writing on the sticky notes, detailing her story illustrations.

Ms. Shannon was documenting the story of one of her students. The student was dictating and Ms. Shannon was writing everything down, asking questions for clarification, and talking to her about her story.

Dallashia approached me. "I'm ready to share my story." She was the child who had shared the story about the ghost earlier. She had finished making her story and was ready to go public with it. Dallashia sat down in a chair facing me and started her Maker's Talk, "reading" from her two drawings. She had continued to hack, repurpose, and grow her story while I was wandering in other Makerspaces of the classroom.

I was in the bed sleeping. There you see me. (*She points to the picture.*) There was a blue ghost. My mommy was with Gwendolyn. Trying not to . . . Mommy was trying to get out. And there was a real ghost. And they were stuck in the house. And the bed was purple. And the whole thing was purple. And my face was purple. Scared.

She got her next piece of paper and continued pointing and turning it all around as she resumed "reading" her story:

Dallashia used colors and details in her illustration to make her story.

And then, once upon a time I went into the restaurant. It was sunny. And we had three plates. Pizza. Mommy was blue. Chicky. And Daddy. And we ran out. And we had some fun. Gwendolyn missed the restaurant because she was late. Because her stomach was hurting. There was a bug. The bug said, "I don't eat it."

There were stories being made in every nook and cranny of the classroom. Every child was engaged. The students were playing and using materials in creative and novel ways to represent characters, settings, and actions as they made their stories. They used language to talk about and share their stories, the emotions they had represented with colors, and their material choices. They were learning through play. They were StoryMaking.

STORYMAKING AND TWENTY-FIRST-CENTURY LEARNING

There is much discussion today that students need to be taught different skills than in the past. Twenty-first-century learning and living will require much more than simply acquiring skills and completing fill-in-the-blank applications. Students will need to know how to think, problem solve, ask questions, persevere, observe carefully, work with others, represent their thoughts, wonder, be creative, and communicate effectively. Enactment of these practices is more than memorization or rote skills. Each practice requires deep thinking and is representative of the dispositions that the current research cites as necessary for competence in the twenty-first century (Ray and Glover 2008; Ritchhart 2015). We need to move students from knowledgeable to "knowledge-able," from being meaning seekers to meaning makers (Wesch 2013).

As you can see in the classroom described earlier, StoryMaking equips young children for the twenty-first century through purposeful play. The children were working alone, in pairs, in small groups. They were learning through play: imagining new stories; tinkering with materials; using materials as representations in stories; building on existing stories; and growing stories by adding color, details, and emotions to their illustrations. The students operated in cultures of StoryMaking and inquiry, making stories collaboratively, seeking out friends' suggestions, repurposing their stories after trial run-throughs, and reflecting during think time. They were having conversations, taking turns, sharing materials, discussing options, trying new materials, representing their thinking, persevering through multiple versions, hacking and repurposing, and exclaiming with wonder and excitement. They were making the stories of their lives.

The children were playing with intention, using multimodal texts (language, art, acting, connecting, drawing, collage), engaging in oral language use, using new words, increasing vocabulary knowledge, meeting state literacy standards, and expanding their literacies, all so they could continue to make and share their everyday stories. They were connecting with one another, school, and their lives. They were StoryMaking.

MAKING MEANING THROUGH STORYMAKING

StoryMaking integrates many areas of learning, including the maker movement, literacy, play, oral language, uses of materials and tools, and more.

Research points to the importance of oral language development in the continuum of literacy learning for young children, but oral language is not the only means by which early learners make meaning and communicate that meaning.

The term *multimodality* "describes approaches to representation which assume that communication and meaning making are about more than just languages" (Flewitt 2013, 296). If you believe that children derive meaning from a variety of sources (environment, television, conversations, stories, pictures, computer games, songs, cartoons) and the modes of communicating this meaning can take many forms (tantrums, song, dance, painting, drawing, computer graphics), then you have a general understanding of multimodality. Multimodality does not discredit oral language as a means for communication but broadens the scope of meaning making and communication beyond oral language to include many languages, or modes, such as props, movement, music, and sculpture.

Rafael makes his story using paint.

StoryMaking builds the bridge between traditional literacy learning and multimodal learning. It addresses state and national standards and expectations for schooled literacy development and use (phonemic awareness, phonics, reading, writing, oral language), while honoring multimodal possibilities and transactions (gesture, painting, building, sculpture) to create a more inclusive culture of learning for all students. After all, "narrative imagining—story—is the fundamental instrument of thought" (Turner 1996, 5). It is our responsibility as educators to build cultures that make it possible for all students to engage in deep thinking and learning as they become literate. StoryMaking, with making as a central focus, provides access points for all children to learn and has led to increased literacy proficiency for our students.

Kaden shares his story in the puppet theater.

StoryMaking is grounded in the transactions between a child, a text, and a story (Rosenblatt 1978). These transactions take place naturally during play, which serves as the conduit for learning for young children. The "text" in StoryMaking is broadly interpreted beyond simply words on a page to include a variety of materials and modes of communication. The story, resulting from the play between the child and the materials (text), includes sharing, or going public. The languages used for going public can include any of the Hundred Languages referred to by Loris Malaguzzi, such as drawing, sewing, painting, sculpting, weaving, dramatic play, music, and dance (Edwards, Gandini, and Forman 1998). These multimodal languages are accompanied by the child's interpretation of the story, thus employing oral language in addition to the many graphic languages (Katz 1998) to share the story.

THE STORYMAKER CYCLE

When we started our journey, we were curious about how we could use the interactive model of the maker movement and its STEAM-related projects to engage children in literacy outcomes. We needed a teaching and learning model that would provide children with a consistent way to work and play that was natural to their learning and a framework from which teachers could plan instruction according to students' needs and curiosities. There are currently many representations for learning practices and criteria within which learners qualify as makers and environments count as Makerspaces. Our StoryMaker Cycle mimics components found in others' work (McGalliard 2016; Resnick 2016; Gauntlett and Thomsen 2013; Brahms and Wardrip 2017; Wohlwend 2013b; MacKay 2013) and adds what and how we have seen our students engage in StoryMaking. Our children imagine, play, make, and share their stories. Often there is crossover between these parts of the cycle, seamless and not-so-seamless transitions, and fluid lines between them. We have tried to categorize our observations and thinking, but the entire process of StoryMaking is recursive, not hierarchal. The children go back and forth, up and down, shallow and deep, and we simply try to follow and keep up with them!

One of the challenges associated with the maker movement is its exclusivity in determining who qualifies as a maker—who is in and who is out. In contrast, Story-Making creates an inclusive community, as each student has unique experiences, families, histories, and stories. No one is without a story. It is through the making of a story that our students come to know themselves and one another. The process, or making, can illuminate the components that matter in their stories; allow time and space for the children to figure out what parts need to be included and how the parts fit together; and provide opportunities for checking affordances of materials, trying out hypotheses, and changing the characters, settings, and plots. StoryMaking empowers students to make their own stories.

Below is an explanation of our observations, accompanied by examples showing why we chose these particular categories to represent our StoryMaker Cycle.

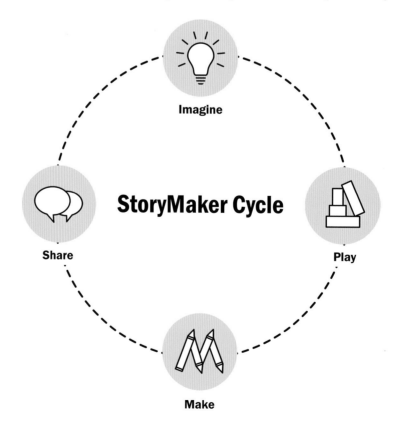

Imagine

Foremost as we begin our StoryMaking journey is setting the stage for the engagement of students' and teachers' imaginations. This is when you plan possibilities for uses of materials, designs for spaces, and lessons that invite wonder and imagination. By employing your own imagination to inspire learning and curiosity, you model to children that imagining is a valid way to begin to learn and play.

Children's imaginations are first engaged by your inspirations: focus lessons, provocations, new materials, beautiful spaces, mentor texts, and more. Then their imaginations are ignited by playing with materials. Children initially may have to play with materials and one another before they can begin to actually imagine their stories. At first you may hear, "How can I use these materials?" But eventually you will hear, "Oh, I have an idea. I need to use this in my story!"

You will know children are using their imaginations when they add their own ideas during their interactions with focus lessons ("I'm going to begin my story with 'One sunny day.'"); imagine new possibilities and innovations with materials ("This is not a wooden craft stick, it's the wall to my house."); and make unique stories that reflect their lives and dreams. Once children understand the StoryMaking process and have engaged in StoryMaking over a period of time, their imaginations will quickly become engaged at the beginning of the StoryMaker Cycle. After all, "among children's greatest strengths is their ability to imagine what is possible" (Brahms and Wardrip 2017, 17).

Focus Lessons in the StoryMaker Cycle

Our students have benefitted from invitations to use their imaginations during explicit focus lessons that inspire wonder and address a need. Remember, focus lessons are short lessons, typically five to fifteen minutes long, that have a learning purpose or goal. The students' interests and curiosities are considered in the choices you will make in the selection and planning for focus lessons. These lessons enable you to create a learning community that has a shared language, common ways of working, and time for shared experiences and understandings. In other words, inviting children to use their imaginations during focus lessons taught to the whole group builds an inclusive learning community for all students.

Focus lessons can target both standards and processes. Often students need mini-lessons that align with specific literacy goals of StoryMaking, such as how to start a story, add details, and use new vocabulary from the writers' world. Story-Making focus lessons can also address particular state standards, such as phases of writing (how to use drawings as a source for ideas, how to use drawings to communicate meaning); storytelling (how to use tone of voice to be a character, how to express characters' emotions); and social-emotional learning (how to give a compliment, how to make helpful comments, how to make a story together).

Focus lessons can also be used to target processes. Children need explicit lessons on routines (how to select materials, how to put away materials, how to use each space) and uses of tools and materials (how to weave using fabric scraps, how to mix paints, how to use a low-temperature glue gun).

Children's stories can be richer when they are initially given the opportunity to engage their imaginations through scaffolded and explicit teaching that is directed at their interests and needs. The children are still invited to explore and play, but the mini-lessons provide a focus on which to anchor their work each day, prior to playing and making their stories.

Play

Play is the overarching context for the transactions that occur between children and their materials. "Children's play worlds are storied worlds with texts filled with vibrant dialogue, characters, and storylines. During play, children make their own imaginary versions of real-life or fantasy worlds but on their own terms, which allows them to make friendships and remake stories to fit their needs" (Wohlwend 2013b, vii). StoryMaking creates spaces that encourage children to imagine, play, make, and share the stories of their lives.

As children begin to play, they select Makerspaces, tools, and materials; determine whether to remake an existing story or begin a new story; and explore the objects and story possibilities. All this requires our youngest learners to employ complex thinking strategies, empowers them to determine the affordances of different materials in conveying their stories, and provides space for flexible thinking as they grow their stories. The teacher can check in during play to monitor progress, scaffold appropriately, and meet needs as they arise. We detail options for checking in in chapter 7.

Make

StoryMaking is so named because as they build the stories of their everyday lives, children enact the practices evidenced in maker movement communities. Researchers have developed a framework describing the learning practices embodied during participation in making (Wardrip and Brahms 2015; Brahms and Crowley 2016). We have used this framework to identify the learning practices our early learners engage in during StoryMaking. Each practice named in the research is listed below, followed by a description of that practice in StoryMaking and specific examples from our StoryMakers as they bring their stories to life.

Inquire. Young children are naturally curious about their worlds. Their imaginations come into play as they explore everyday tools, materials, and spaces. StoryMaking begins as children question and wonder about their worlds, their lives, and themselves. The goal in starting StoryMaking with inspirations to ignite their imaginations is to get children to begin to inquire: "How does that work?" "Why did it do that?" "What materials can I use for my pizza restaurant?" "How can I build my castle for my story?"

Express intention. Initially in StoryMaking, children's goals are simple and pertain to selecting spaces and materials for play. After the focus lesson or another provocation you use to ignite their imaginations, you might ask your children where they want to play or what materials they want to use in their play. It may sound like, "Celeste, where are you going to make your story today?" or "Raul, yesterday you were working in blocks to make your fire engine story. Do you want to return to blocks or make your story with another material?" Many times, the children's plans and intentions change as they play, and there are several strategies you can use to help them stay with their plans, which we'll explore in chapter 5.

Two children share their plans drawn on a sticky note.

Tinker, test, and iterate. Once children have played and familiarized themselves with the uses and affordances of particular materials, they begin to explore and test the materials to decide whether particular materials will fit the needs of their stories. Zachariah, one of our students, played for a long time with the collage materials. First he used glass stones to represent his friends and family in the story he was making. After tinkering with some of the other materials and with his story, he decided that colorful fluff balls worked much better to represent his friends and family. They were "prettier" and "looked more like them." He later used the glass stones as treetops in his story. He tinkered, tested, and figured out which materials best represented the story elements in the story he was making. Tinkering typically occurs during Phase 1, "Explore," of our inquiry framework (see pages 57–58).

You will recognize students engaged in tinkering and testing practices when you observe them playing and notice that they seem to be using a particular material and then trading it out for another, switching back and forth between materials. Or they may start in housekeeping and then take some of their materials to another Makerspace and set them up again, adding new materials from the new space. They are thinking stories into existence as they StoryMake, tinkering and testing out possibilities.

Seek out resources. During StoryMaking, children seek out resources to get ideas, ask for feedback, and make their stories better. Resources are everywhere in a room full of young learners. Children can serve as resources, offering expertise, opinions, and compliments about one another's ideas, materials, and stories. For example, Nathan kept inserting pipe cleaners into Yostin's story. Nathan was quite sure that Yostin's story would be much better if Yostin used pipe cleaners for rain instead of the wooden craft sticks Yostin had selected. Eventually, after they worked together and talked about the story, Yostin used a pipe cleaner to represent a snake in his story. Their conversation included vocabulary about snakes, figuring out how to shape the pipe cleaner to make it look like a snake, and studying the shape of a snake in an illustration in a mentor text to make sure their pipe cleaner accurately represented a snake. When the children use one another as resources during Story-Making, richer and more robust stories and learning result.

Materials and tools can be resources, serving to ensure the stories children make accurately represent their thinking. Anchor charts are one of the most valuable tools our children use as a resource; these are charts that you create collaboratively with the students during focus lessons to anchor their thinking. They can show where story ideas come from, ways to begin a story, or the StoryMaker Cycle with pictures of the students and their stories in each phase of the cycle. Anchor charts can be removed after the children have gained fluency with the information the charts contain, and new anchor charts can be posted as you teach new information about

StoryMaking. You will find examples of various types of anchor charts throughout the book.

Another example of using materials as resources can be seen when one of our students, Jasmine, wanted to use puppets in her castle story, but she could not find a puppet with brown hair like hers. She wandered the classroom looking for something that would work for her puppet's hair. Finally she came across some yarn with tassles. Perfect! She cut the yarn and taped it to the puppet's head. She used the material as a resource to more accurately represent her story. Resources can serve multiple purposes in StoryMaking and are in abundance in spaces where there are lots of early learners!

Hack and repurpose. Once a StoryMaker has made a story, Phase 2, "Investigate," of the inquiry framework is initiated (see pages 59–60). "Investigate" is the time children's learning grows deeper, when they decide whether to grow their existing stories or start new stories. The purpose of this phase is for children to try different versions of their story (revising) by repurposing materials.

Growing a story can take many forms, but it can include adding details, trying different materials to make the story more closely depict what they imagined, or using a new tool or material to enhance the story. You will recognize when children are growing a story when they continue to work on it over time, often after they have shared it with you or their classmates. For example, Christian thought he was finished with his story about a big storm, but then he decided to add his aunt and uncle, and then he added his cousins, and then the house needed to be bigger. He grew his story over several days, and when he was ready to share it again, it had more details, characters, and actions.

Sometimes StoryMakers hack and repurpose entire stories, creating a new story. You may recognize this when you see children knock down an entire tower of blocks they've been working on and start building something different. Children often start with a clean slate by getting rid of their first story or attempt. For example, Alicia was making a story about her family in collage, but none of the materials was the right shape for her dog. She moved to the clay Makerspace and used playdough so she could have more control over the shape of the dog. A menagerie of playdough animal characters was created, the setting was changed to a forest, and the resulting story was completely different. The original story had been hacked and repurposed.

Because children are not always aware of the purpose or intent of a particular material, they more easily hack its original intent, adapt it for their own purposes, and use it according to the needs of their story.

Develop fluency. As children engage in StoryMaking each day, they quickly become knowledgeable about the uses of tools and materials, your StoryMaking routines and expectations, and the StoryMaker Cycle. Children need time and practice to develop fluency, so establishing a designated time for StoryMaking in your schedule is a good start to ensuring they become proficient. Children need forty-five to sixty minutes each day for playing and making stories to develop familiarity with materials, practice using them, and innovate with them. You will find that young learners get frustrated if they have to start cleaning up just as they're becoming deeply engaged in playing and making.

You will recognize that learners have developed fluency with materials and tools when they use them appropriately and start to innovate with them. For example, when first introduced to tape, Mario had it strung out everywhere and stuck to everything. He needed time to practice pulling it on the roll, tearing a piece off, and figuring out how to use it to stick more than one material together. Once he developed fluency with masking tape, he was able to use duct tape, invisible tape, and two-sided tape to meet his needs. He became a resource to others in the uses of tape. He even innovated with tape, forming a bird with colorful duct tape to represent a bird character in his story. Children can become master carpenters, bakers, and pediatricians, both in the classroom and in their stories, when they are given time and space to develop fluency and expertise.

Simplify to complexify. In StoryMaking, children often use simple materials to make complex stories. They complexify. For instance, Sanchez used two simple materials, pipe cleaners and plastic beads, and made a magnificent sculpture that represented his story, his life. Complexifying in StoryMaking becomes evident over time. Students first develop fluency with the uses of tools, materials, and StoryMaking. Then, with proficiency, they more easily innovate and are able to complexify their uses and representations. They combine materials from a variety of spaces for one story. They take familiar materials, such as tree branches and twigs, and combine them with other materials to build their unique stories. The resulting stories include simple materials serving multiple purposes in the context of story, complexified to match the complex stories our children are living and thinking into existence each day.

StoryMaking occurs through the enactment of the learning practices of making: inquire, plan, tinker, seek out resources, hack and repurpose, develop fluency, and complexify. As children become StoryMakers, they discover their stories, themselves, and the many literacies and materials available to them to make sense of their worlds.

Share

This is the time in StoryMaking when children share their stories (or go public), invite feedback from their peers if they're stuck, employ listening strategies, and provide compliments to one another. During StoryMaking each day, children may choose to share their stories with you or a partner, with several friends, or with the entire class. Informal sharing can take place anytime during the StoryMaker Cycle, but whole class share time is usually at the end of StoryMaking each day. We refer to this time as Maker's Talks. Just as science talks help children communicate and reflect on their experiences and new ideas and focus their thinking on the science concepts and processes, the same is true in the literacy context of StoryMaking. We provide time daily for children to reflect on the stories they made, how they made them, and what they were thinking as they made their stories.

Not all children are comfortable participating in Maker's Talks, as they may not be confident in or able to use oral language to communicate. During share time, children may choose to share their stories using any one of the Hundred Languages of Loris Malaguzzi (1998). They may share their stories through dance, singing, signing, pointing—whatever works for them to convey their stories. Even though we give students time to communicate each day, it is during Phase 3, "Communicate," of our inquiry framework that we teach explicit lessons on possibilities for publishing, or going public (see page 61).

Because students are encouraged to select materials of their choice to create stories of their choice and present them in languages of their choice, sharing always includes a variety of ways to communicate. StoryMaking creates an inclusive community that celebrates each story.

> **• Voices from the Field •**
>
> "I LOVE IT! Having implemented this in my classroom last year, I was amazed at the growth I saw in my students. Even the quietest, most reserved students (including my ELL students) were excited about sharing their stories. They took risks that continuously surprised me, and their stories were *amazing!*"
>
> —Shannon, pre-K teacher

TIPS FOR STUDENTS WITH SPECIAL RIGHTS

Play is much like reading in that it appears simple but is actually a complex endeavor during which deep learning occurs. The National Association for the Education of Young Children's position statement about developmentally appropriate practice asserts that "play is an important vehicle for developing self-regulation as well as for promoting language, cognition, and social competence" (NAEYC 2009, 14). Most people assume that all children naturally know how to play, but some children do not, and StoryMaking has also served as the context for teaching students with special rights *how* to play. Here are some tips on how to include children with special rights in StoryMaking:

- Start with explicit lessons about how to play, modeling and creating interactive lessons that are accessible to all children. It may sound something like this example from teacher Rachel: "I really like the farm set. Watch me play with the farm toys. This reminds me of when I went to the farm with my family. I saw the farmer feed the cow. The cow enjoyed the hay and said, 'Moo.' Jessica, can you help the farmer feed the cow?" A student in need of this type of instruction would more than likely be working on imitation as a foundation for learning, so you could ask the child to copy your actions.

- Don't limit students' possibilities for sharing. Allow them to use any language to convey their stories, whatever enables success for the learner. Sally had a nonverbal student in her classroom who had trouble communicating his story. She took pictures of his family and different settings (like the beach, a store, a house) and added some additional pictures of common household items. She narrated the story as he arranged the pictures in a sequence. If she said something that he did not intend, he shook his head "no." He shared his story by pointing to the pictures as Sally narrated: "One day, I went to the beach with my family. We used a shovel to dig in the sand. We gathered shells." Sally continually added new pictures from which he could choose to make his stories. His mom would send in pictures when they had new adventures and visited new places so he could expand his story repertoire.

FINAL THOUGHTS

After reading this chapter, we hope that you understand how StoryMaking has the potential to grow your children's literacies while engaging them in the learning practices of the maker movement. In our district StoryMaking has provided a framework for expanding the multimodal literacies of our students; created an inclusive space in which all children have access to these multimodal literacies; demonstrated the value of play in the learning processes of young children; and provided an opportunity for observing children's play and engagement in the learning practices of making. We can't wait to share what we've learned with you so your children will have opportunities to enact the stories of their lives through the imagine, play, make, and share processes of the StoryMaker Cycle.

Maker's Moment

Ms. Rachel introduced a new material to support her children in imagining new stories. She provided foam blocks to build and paint to stamp their stories. After time to tinker with the materials and repurpose their use, Averie, Kimberly, and Amayah made a story that they were proud to share:

"Once upon a time, there was three girls playing in a castle. There was just princesses no queens. They run away because there was thunder."—Amayah

"First, we built the castle and then we painted it. Averie, Kimberly, and me built the castle."—Amayah

CHAPTER 2

An Environment *Made* for StoryMaking

CREATING A PLAYFUL ENVIRONMENT FOR STORYMAKING

A few weeks into the school year, Michelle was just beginning a lesson introducing a new Makerspace, attachments, to inspire stories in Ms. Shannon's classroom. She first brought out a box of materials and asked aloud, "Hmmm, let's see. What materials do I have here?" She pulled out one item at a time and named a clothespin, tie wrap, binder clip, piece of cardboard, rubber band, tape, ruler, and sticks.

The students had been playing with materials and one another as they were engaged in making their stories in their Makerspaces (housekeeping, blocks, library, science, art) during the first few weeks of the school year. These new materials that Michelle was introducing seemed to puzzle them. Then Michelle asked, "What could I make with these materials?" She also posted some pictures of structures created out of sticks and other natural loose parts.

One image resembled a boat, and Michelle explained that she was going to try out this idea. She began making her boat in front of the students. She pulled two sticks out of the pile and wondered how she was going to attach the pieces together. "Use tape!" one student suggested. Michelle got a piece of tape and wrapped it tightly around the two sticks. All faces lifted with this successful operation just as the pieces fell apart. "That's okay. We just need to find the right materials to make the boat." Michelle explained her thinking processes while modeling persistence and problem-solving skills. She continued in this way for a few minutes, trying rubber bands to hold the sticks together to form the base of the boat, clothespins as the people, and a tie wrap for a paddle.

Michelle said, "This reminds me of a time I went canoeing with my husband, Shawn." She had been imagining possibilities for a story as she explored the materials. As she continued to play with the materials and make her story, she

A Makerspace anchor chart helps remind children of the possibilities they've learned about.

labeled her actions, describing why she was choosing certain materials for the parts of the story that these materials had unlocked in her memory. Michelle eventually sat up proudly and said, "I'm ready to share my story!" The students leaned in as they listened to Michelle share her story with her canoe creation. She acted out her story as she shared: "One windy day, Shawn and I went to Myakka River State Park to go canoeing. We paddled far out into the lake. Just then the wind began to blow us farther out. Shawn said, 'Paddle!' I tried. One stroke, two strokes, and then the wind blew us back. I tried again. One stroke, two strokes, and then the wind blew us back. There were alligators all around. My arms were so tired. But with Shawn doing most of the paddling, we finally made it back to the dock. Shawn said it would be a long time before he took me canoeing again. The end!" Michelle paused and the children burst into applause.

Michelle explained that because she used her imagination as she played with the materials, they had unlocked a memory for a story to make and share.

Then it was time for the students to decide what materials they wanted to explore. Gryffin said he wanted to go to housekeeping "because we have cups and I made juice with my mom once." Even visualizing and talking about the uses of materials in a Makerspace that Gryffin knew very well was igniting his imagination and memory for a story. He didn't have all the details for his story, but he expressed his vision to act out and try on this story about making juice with the materials in housekeeping. That is the power of play. That is the power of materials.

StoryMaking environments provide children with the time, materials, tools, and space to imagine, play, make, and share the everyday stories of their lives. Below we discuss each of the components for setting up an environment conducive to StoryMaking. We will start with time, setting up schedules to include StoryMaking. We then discuss materials. Finally, we introduce Makerspaces we have in our classrooms and the corresponding materials found in each of these spaces.

MAKING TIME FOR STORYMAKING

In our learning communities, teachers have found there are many ways to arrange their schedules to include StoryMaking time. Our full-day classrooms usually have two opportunities for explore time (also known as choice time or free-play time) in their days. Typically, one session is scheduled in the morning and the other is scheduled in the afternoon. If you have this type of schedule, then you could decide to turn one of your explore times into StoryMaking. Other teachers have chosen both a morning and an afternoon time to schedule their StoryMaking. All have been successful. Consider the needs of your children and your preferences when making your schedule.

If most of your children attend only in the morning or if you have a half-day program, then your main explore or free-play time would become StoryMaking.

However you are creating your schedule, you will need to balance the amount of free-play and StoryMaking time. We will show you tools for monitoring students' learning in chapter 7.

Regardless of what time of day you schedule your StoryMaking, it will be important to provide your children with lots of time to use their imaginations, play, and make their stories. StoryMaking can occur anytime during the day, but we have found through trial and error that it works best for our students and teachers if it is part of explore time. Most of our teachers initially offered "story" as one of the options during explore time. Now the students look forward to StoryMaking time and use materials as they play in many of the areas. In *Purposeful Play*, Kristine Mraz, Alison Porcelli, and Cheryl Tyler (2016) recommend forty-five to sixty minutes each day, five days per week, for their workshop approach, including choice time with pre-K students. Less time than that does not give children an opportunity to get immersed in their work (play). We typically break it down like this:

- Imagine (focus lesson with provocation, exemplar, or introduction to new material): 5–10 minutes

- Play & Make: 35–40 minutes

- Share: 5–10 minutes

Students will be engaged for even longer periods of time once they have explored the uses of the materials, established routines, learned the components of Story-Making, and built perseverance.

It is important to give children plenty of time to interact with the materials before expecting them to make their stories. You will have a room full of frustrated children if you give them only a few minutes to play and make. They will have had only enough time to become immersed in their playing and making before it is time to clean up. This is one way StoryMaking can stall.

MATERIALS FOR STORYMAKING

According to Cate Heroman, "Making is using stuff to make stuff" (2017, 4). Materials are the *stuff* of playing and making. The uses of all materials can result in engagement of the senses, curious wonderings, and increased creativity. Ingrid Chalufour and Karen Worth explain: "With carefully selected materials and thoughtful guidance, children's explorations will encourage them to observe more closely, develop new ideas about the world, and build a foundation of experiences and ideas on which to construct later understanding" (2003, 2).

We recommend using materials in the classroom that are open-ended; in other words, materials that do not have a "right" and "wrong" use. One way to kill creativity is to have only one "right" answer for a problem; likewise, if there is only one way to use a material, that material does not encourage imagination. Open-ended materials can be manipulated, explored, and used in many different ways. Research shows that "open-ended toys that lead to high-quality play contribute more to academic outcomes than many educational toys" (Trawick-Smith et al. 2015, 70). Commercial toys and other pop culture items also provide texts for stories, but these materials sometimes have meanings embedded in them so their stories already exist. Using commercial and pop culture items is a step toward growing children's own stories; however, open-ended materials can serve a variety of purposes and invoke curiosity and imagination during StoryMaking.

> **• Voices from the Field •**
>
> "One of the most exciting things is that this [StoryMaking] gives our students an opportunity to explore materials and create freely. They can use their imaginations and make their stories using a variety of materials, and they are not bound by normal conventions. StoryMaking gives them opportunities to expand their oral language vocabulary, improve their storytelling skills, and take risks they might not normally take."
> —Rachel, integrated pre-K teacher

Loose parts, typically natural materials, are gaining popularity with teachers of young children. They are open-ended, can be found in the environment, and can be transported, combined, controlled, categorized, arranged, and manipulated through play. They can become representations for other items and become parts of stories. Some examples include dried leaves, sticks, stones, beads, wooden discs, paper clips, and shells. Loose parts can be used in combination with other materials or put into action by themselves. They are typically used to make collages, to sew or weave together, as tools in painting, and for building. Specific suggestions will be made along the way for possible uses of loose parts during StoryMaking.

Materials used to create a Makerspace may include sticks, tape, clips, rubber bands, and tie wraps.

The materials of the maker movement include everything from crafting supplies (glue, fabric, jewels, wooden craft sticks) to engineering apparatuses (squishy boards, circuits, electronic gadgets). StoryMaking currently focuses on the crafting end of the continuum, as crafting is an easy point of entry for children and adults, offers access to fluency and expertise for young children, and can be a scaffold toward more complex endeavors such as coding and circuitry (Wohlwend, Keune, and Peppler 2016; Fields and Lee 2016).

How Children Engage with Materials during a StoryMaker Cycle

Any material or object can inspire stories. Our worlds are full of stories waiting to be made and brought to life. A cautionary note about our focus on particular materials, as Erika Christakis reminds us: "The materials can easily become . . . an end point of learning rather than the vehicle for it. . . . Classroom materials are there to support the child's engagement with the world. Nothing more and nothing less" (2016, 188). If you do not have access to the materials we've mentioned, then consider your goals for the materials and determine some alternatives. Do not despair. As you will see, children's imaginations do not require expensive materials or the latest toys. Dirt, rocks, sticks, and water are viable and open-ended materials that can be used to make beautiful stories. The suggestions in this chapter are simply that, suggestions and possibilities. Feel free to add your own ideas to ours. Young children will discover found materials, uncover loose parts, and find other unexpected surprises. Celebrate their creativity and ingenuity in finding and using imaginations and materials to make their stories.

Children use reflective materials to play and make stories.

Imagine

There are some simple strategies you can use to engage children's imaginations with the uses of materials. Introducing a new or unusual item and asking the children "What could this be used for when we make our story?" will ignite imaginations. Modeling a different use of a common material can spark imaginations, such as using a banana from the housekeeping space as a phone in the story you are making. An anchor chart may also serve as inspiration by showing different materials accompanied by photographs of students using the materials in their stories.

Play

Our students experienced more ease in playing and making their stories with specific materials. We recommended that our teachers start either by introducing a new material (such as collage or a new type of block) or by observing the materials and spaces their children are the most interested in during play and then growing those spaces and materials.

• Voices from the Field •

"Students expressed much interest in building houses, castles, and bridges. We then began to create an inspiration space with photos of these items built with materials similar to the ones we provided. We will continue to grow this space with pictures of student-created structures and stories."

—Angela, pre-K teacher

As Ann Pelo (2017) states, it is necessary to allow children to first engage all their senses to explore and come to know a material and its characteristics, malleability, and possibilities. When introducing a new material during StoryMaking, we can anticipate that children will initially explore, make a mess, experiment, stack, and dump! Giving children time to investigate and play with materials is paramount to their discovery of the forms and functions of the materials. This is the time during which they will begin to imagine story possibilities and think them into existence.

In addition to providing time for play with materials, you can question the children's uses of materials during play to help them consider story possibilities. For example, ask questions such as "How are you going to use this in your story?" or "I notice you are playing with the blocks. Can you tell me about the block story you are thinking about while you're playing?"

Make

The name StoryMaking implies the use of "real materials, real tools, and authentic processes in ways that are open-ended, exploratory, iterative, and self-directed. . . . This begins with making familiar materials accessible to children and encouraging them to engage with materials in new ways" (Brahms and Wardrip 2016).

After the students have explored a new material with all their senses, they may be ready to explore the possibilities of representation with the new material; in other words, they can start to *make* their stories. This is when children move from pretend play to symbolic play, using objects and language to represent ideas (Hamlin and Wisneski 2012). Children are invited to select materials and use them to represent people, places, and things in their stories. You will recognize that children are making when they begin to put objects together and narrate their actions, or when they move from place to place gathering materials for their stories. Often making consists of children building structures, putting together materials, or gathering stuff in one locale.

After a while, given time and space, the children may be ready to remake their story using another medium or material. This is Phase 2 of the inquiry cycle. The children can then compare affordances, notice limitations, and determine the best means by which to convey their stories. In other words, they can select the best materials for their particular stories (Kress 2013; Pelo 2017; Wohlwend 2008). Children sometimes surprise themselves, grow their stories, and develop different paths when they remake their stories using a new material. Our students move freely from one space to another as they play and make and remake their stories.

Share

Children finally use materials to communicate their stories. They share the collages, drawings, structures, dances, or sculptures they have made individually or with their friends. They employ oral language to tell their stories or use any one of the other Hundred Languages referred to in *The Hundred Languages of Children* (Edwards, Gandini, and Forman 1998). Options for sharing are provided in chapter 6.

Children use their imaginations and think deeply about their stories through play with materials, make their stories over time and with various materials, and share the stories they've created both individually and collaboratively. The process of imagining, playing, making, and sharing employs standards across the curriculum, from social-emotional development to approaches to learning, from language development to creative arts, and so on.

THE SPACES AND MATERIALS
FOR STORYMAKING

Below are recommendations about the spaces you can set up for StoryMaking and materials you can place in your already existing spaces that will contribute to StoryMaking. The materials and spaces can scaffold your students toward proficiency with both the uses of materials and StoryMaking. While the natural inclination for most of us is to order the technology, tools, and materials first, Laura Fleming warns us that "it is the planning that takes the most time and focus" (2015, 13). Our purpose is to inspire your planning in the design of your spaces and the materials that you place in those spaces. Keep in mind that the most important consideration in your planning should be the interests and needs of your children.

The placement, display, and uses of materials are a vital part of the environment for StoryMaking success. Children can use all sorts of materials and spaces to make their stories, but some spaces and materials offer easier ways to represent characters, settings, conflicts, and feelings. Some spaces and materials inspire imagination and appeal to young children more than other spaces. Your goals and objectives for StoryMaking will drive particular selections of materials in your Makerspaces. As you consider the suggestions below, think about your purposes and select the materials and spaces that align with your goals for your children. Here are some tips in placing materials in your spaces:

- Place materials where students can see them and access them. Some of our teachers used baskets and placed them at or below children's eye level; others used clear plastic boxes.

- Display pictures of stories at each Makerspace or area. For example, when a child makes a story out of blocks, take a photograph and dictation of the story. Post the picture with the transcription at the block area. These students' exemplars will serve to ignite other children's imaginations and will honor the stories of the children.

A teacher uses photo documentation to inspire stories.

Once you introduce a material, leave it out for an extended period, as the children's uses and representations became more detailed over time. However, if you never change the materials, then the children will lose interest. We recommend changing with each unit of study, or about every six to nine weeks. If you notice your students losing interest prior to that amount of time, add a new material to pique their interest or add a new Makerspace to your environment. This will keep your students engaged and provide the time they need to develop detailed stories.

We started StoryMaking in our regular explore stations, renaming them *Makerspaces* as the children became more intentional with their uses of the materials to make their stories in these spaces. We slowly added more Makerspaces as the children gained fluency in the uses of materials, tools, and spaces. There is no need to create Makerspaces separate from your other areas during StoryMaking, as all stations or areas in your classroom can become Makerspaces. Below are spaces and materials typically found in early childhood settings that can become Makerspaces for StoryMaking.

Blocks

Blocks can be a good place to begin StoryMaking. The students use blocks to physically and literally build or make their stories. There are many different options for types of blocks available for classroom use, and children can use all sorts of blocks to make and grow their stories. Building blocks offer a natural invitation to build collaborative stories. Even when children are building individual stories with their blocks, the structures often intersect and stories are joined. Stories become collaborative ventures.

When asked later what material they'd started with, each of our teachers said they'd selected blocks to begin the year. If you start to introduce your materials at the beginning of the year, and are opening one station, space, or area at a time, then a block center gives you multiple options. Blocks can be the start of making and eventually can become a Makerspace. There are numerous types of blocks, and they are always a favorite with all our children. If you can't decide which kind of block to start with, hardwood unit blocks are a good choice: "One simple open-ended toy scored higher than all others: . . . hardwood unit blocks. . . . Blocks inspire construction, make-believe, artistic expression, motor play, and sorting and categorizing. We also found that children's language and social interactions improved more when playing with unit blocks than with any other toy" (Trawick-Smith et al. 2015, 71).

We suggest that you have multiple types of blocks to give students options in their StoryMaking. You could introduce a specific type of block and model making a story with that type, or place multiple options in the block space and see what the students do with them. One of the characteristics of the maker movement is the use of authentic materials and tools. When blocks become a Makerspace, we include real wood blocks, wood discs, wood scraps, and real tools such as hammers, screwdrivers, and sandpaper. We also introduce different types of blocks throughout the year. This allows the block Makerspace to remain engaging for our children.

Initially children may more easily manipulate large blocks that are lightweight, such as cardboard "brick" blocks, hardwood hollow blocks, and big foam blocks. When children are learning to add details to their stories, you can introduce texture and color to the blocks (bristle blocks, specimen viewing blocks, color window blocks, Magna-Tiles, crystal building blocks, translucent light and color tabletop blocks, mirror blocks). Natural settings can be enhanced in stories with the introduction of nature blocks, wooden unit blocks, architectural unit blocks, log blocks, Dr. Drew's Discovery Blocks, Kapla blocks, or bamboo building blocks. If your focus is on characters, Legos can be used to create all sorts of people and animals.

One of our teachers taught her students how to play in the block area during her mornings. When it was time for StoryMaking during the afternoon, she simply said, "We are going to use the same materials from the block area this morning, but now we can make a story." Ms. Shannon quickly modeled a story with some of the blocks. The children went off to play, and she could hear some of them saying, "My story is about . . ." and "I'm using this for my story." StoryMaking is a natural process for children and adults alike. When we play, memories and stories are unlocked, and sometimes we are willing to tell them aloud. As teachers, we need to recognize these mini-stories, capture them, and praise the children for their storytelling skills!

Sculpting

Sculpting Makerspaces include playdough, modeling clay, aluminum foil, and different gauges and varieties of wire, including colors, sizes, and textures of pipe cleaners, floral wire, and coated wire. These Makerspaces may have tools for carving, imprinting, and cutting playdough, as well as objects that can be used to press designs into clay. Plastic utensils work well for cutting playdough, while cutting tools for wire include scissors and snippers.

Most environments for early learners include a space for play with playdough, which provides easy access to sculpting possibilities and works toward addressing many standards. As it tends to get stuck in carpet, playdough is best used where there is a floor that can be swept and scraped. Some of our teachers use cookie trays as the background for playdough stories, providing a neat space for play and a nice story setting.

Research by Mallary Swartz outlines the developmental abilities and learning concepts addressed by play with playdough, including the domains of language development, literacy, and approaches to learning (2005, 102–3). Imagine the possibilities when children play with playdough *and* stories!

Introducing clay after playdough is the next step in the progression of working with three-dimensional sculpting materials. As with the introduction of any new material, the children will need a chance to explore and investigate the forms and functions of clay. After they have played with its texture, pliancy, and wetness, children will be ready to begin working with it to form their stories and sculptures. This is when the children begin to use the clay to represent their stories in the making.

We introduce wire, including different gauges and a variety of metals, last. To help children initially form shapes, provide pencils, dowels, or anything the children can use to wrap the wire around and make curlicues or coils. Pliers, a new tool, can then be introduced to and used by young children to shape the wire. Once children have learned to shape wire, they can figure out ways to connect it. Then they can string beads on it, lace it with feathers, and wrap it around other loose parts to add dimension and texture (Pelo 2017).

Below are some tips for working with specific sculpting materials:

- Demonstrate how to use tools to roll and cut the clay.

- Show how to roll the clay flat and use the surface as a canvas to carve a story in the clay.

- Be sure to teach the children to tape the pointed ends of the wire to keep from getting jabbed by them.

Children use foil to sculpt characters for their stories.

Housekeeping/Dramatic Play

"Children learn by playing with everyday objects and by pretending. The old stand-bys of water, sand, mixing bowls, and cardboard boxes are still the most effective ways for babies and young children to learn about the physical world, while the whole world of pretend—dolls and costumes and toy dishes—is the most effective way to learn about the social world" (Gopnik 2010, 26). The housekeeping and dramatic play Makerspaces are full of such materials that invite stories. Materials can be rotated, new provocations can be introduced, and authentic materials can be used naturally in these areas of the classroom. When possible, include real cereal boxes, soup cans, utensils, clothing, houseplants, and accessories in the kitchen, dramatic play, and housekeeping areas. Authentic materials serve multiple purposes: a real spoon can of course serve as a spoon in a restaurant scene, but it can also be used as a measuring stick in a building scenario, a tongue depressor at a vet's office, a telephone in a conversation, and a drumstick in a band presentation.

Drawing and Painting

In *The Language of Art*, Ann Pelo (2017) recommends that teachers start with drawing and coloring prior to introducing watercolor. First crayons, then markers, then paints. There are also continuums for brushes, types of paints, and types of paper. We start with crayons. We also discovered watercolor pencils, then moved into paint, followed by oil pastels.

Below are some tips for providing art materials:

- Begin with crayons and colored pencils, which will allow children to draw details.

- When introducing paint, provide small brushes so children can draw facial features and other details.

- Limit the amount of paint so children do not become overwhelmed by the number of choices. Our teachers have used muffin tins to pour small amounts of a variety of colors of paint. The tins are also stable, so paint won't spill as easily as it can in small cups.

- Change the types of paper (finger painting, watercolor, card stock) along with the type of art medium to keep areas engaging.

Collage

We introduced collage as the first new addition to our regular Makerspaces. Although we recommend rotating materials, inserting new provocations, and making changes to keep the learners engaged, collage has become a permanent Makerspace option in our classrooms. We created additional and simultaneous Makerspaces, but collage remained open throughout the year. The students love working with loose parts, found materials, and other bits and pieces to make their stories.

Collage is an easy and engaging "language" that can be used to make stories. The background or base for collage can be construction paper, foam sheets, felt sheets, or whatever else may be available that invites children to engage and make their stories. Our teachers have collected placemats, enlarged photographs, and purchased scrapbook paper with scenes. The collages do not have to be permanently glued down. We have found that not gluing them gives the children opportunities to change their minds, add details, use different representations, and hack and repurpose. We would, however, suggest capturing what the child has made each day by taking anecdotal notes, photographs, or videos of the collage. Ideally students will learn to take their own pictures of their work, but initially an adult will probably have to be responsible for photos and other documentation. The documentation serves as a reminder to the students as they revisit, hack and repurpose, and seek others' opinions. It acts as a scaffold toward next steps, more complex thinking, and continuing to engage in a particular story. See chapter 7 for more on documentation.

Annabel is using documentation from her first story made with collage materials to remake her story and repurpose the materials.

Collage materials used for making stories are often loose parts and can be colorful, recycled, inexpensive, and simple to attain: twigs, sticks, branches, bark, pine needles, pine cones, leaves, dirt, sand, grass, shells, bottle caps, coins, dried beans, yarn, beads, glass gems, marbles, rickrack, stones, pebbles, wood discs, Scrabble pieces, shells, foil, translucent fabric scraps, and metallic objects.

Allow children to transport materials across the room. Although we recommend having a home for each material, students should be able to re-imagine uses and representations of the materials. Sometimes this means mixing it up and combining objects in surprising ways. In a culture of thinking, this is a good thing, although not always neat and organized!

Weaving

Although we weren't sure it would become weaving, we put out some materials that could be used for weaving (or for a variety of other purposes): sticks, twigs, fabric scraps, long strips of cloth, feathers, string, rope, torn paper pieces, twine, yarn, and more. Weaving, like many Makerspaces, can be a solitary process or a collaborative effort that results in a variety of stories, many of which are amended, edited, and hacked as a result of the affordances of materials. Our students typically start with simple lace boards or framed pieces of screen and practice the in and out, up and down, with yarn. They've also engaged in weaving giant structures with sticks, palm fronds, found materials, and fabric scraps. The large weavings afford opportunities for making both multiple small stories within one project and one large collaborative story that combines and complexifies many stories into one. As the children gain proficiency with lace boards and weaving large pieces, they begin to try out more complex types of weaving and sewing.

Andrew weaves his spider story.

Attachments

Anyone who has worked with young children can attest to the fact that children love to use tape and glue of all sorts: glue sticks, school glue, masking tape, invisible tape, duct tape. They also have a fascination with clips, clothespins, paper clips, rubber bands, and other materials used to hold things together or connect things. We first introduced attachments for connecting, using cardboard and sticks as the materials that would be connected. You may choose any type of material for connecting, but sticks were a good choice for us because they caused a lot of problems; children would be making a story, and the sticks would not stay connected—the tape would come undone, or the clips would not fit around the stick's diameter. This became an opportunity for children to problem solve, ask questions, use resources, learn from one another, and get stuck. It was interesting to watch how the stories changed as a result of the materials not doing the jobs for which the original stories intended them. Problem-solving techniques were tried, stories were hacked, and there was sometimes frustration, but ultimately, stories were made. We have also used this space to introduce hammers, pliers, screwdrivers, low-temperature glue guns, and other tools. Some other materials our teachers have placed in their attachments Makerspaces include nuts and bolts, PVC pipes, cups, measuring cups, funnels, hoses, paper tubes, shoeboxes, flashlights, and anything that may support a focus lesson or other activity or unit of study.

HOW DO I BEGIN TEACHING STORYMAKING?

If you are thinking of implementing StoryMaking at the beginning of the year, here are two options for how to begin:

- First open up your classroom by introducing a few areas at a time to establish ways and expectations for playing in the block area, housekeeping, art, and so on. Once you see the students becoming more independent during their play, you can introduce a new way to play in the Makerspaces. You can provide focus lessons on how to play with those same materials for the purpose of making a story.

- A second option is to jump in and begin StoryMaking on day one! We have had teachers share their launching lesson on the first day of school, and StoryMaking is part of the daily routine from the beginning. Introduce only one or two areas at a time with the purpose of making a story.

We will share specific lessons that will help with implementation of both of these options in chapter 4.

TIPS FOR STUDENTS WITH SPECIAL RIGHTS

- Provide opportunities for students who have difficulties with fine-motor skills to StoryMake with larger materials. We have found that the giant blocks and bigger loose parts are easier for some students to manipulate as they make their stories.

- Too many choices of tools and materials can be overwhelming for some children. If you have children who need fewer options, then narrow the possibilities while still providing a choice: "Abby, yesterday you drew your story in the art Makerspace. I've noticed you like to play in collage as well. Would you like to remake it in collage today? Or would you rather stay in art?"

FINAL THOUGHTS

StoryMaking provides avenues for all children to experience success with the uses of tools and materials as they make their stories. Be sure to make the materials accessible to all learners by placing them at a level the children can see and use. Introducing new materials and tools during focus lessons is an engaging invitation to ignite their imaginations as they play and make their stories. Give them time to explore, experiment, and gain fluency with the uses of materials and tools. Proficiency will lead to innovation—and beautiful stories.

Maker's Moment

Michelle noticed Fernando playing with dinosaur toys and loose parts in one of the Makerspaces in the pre-K classroom in the museum. Dinosaur stories had begun to take shape in the classroom since the new dinosaur exhibit arrived at the museum. Michelle invited children who wanted to imagine a dinosaur story to visit the new space. She brought a basket of new loose parts to see what the children would play and make. They took a few minutes to study the exhibit and then discussed how they could start their story by describing the place. This is what they made:

Fernando rehearses his imagined dinosaur story.

"One day, at the dinosaur house, the dinosaurs got loud. 'Roarrr!' We gave him food and a drink of water. Then he ate the food. Everyone got in the water and swam away. Then they went to sleep. The end!"

Creating a StoryMaking Culture through Inquiry

USING DIFFERENT MATERIALS TO REMAKE STORIES

One day in late November, Michelle reflected with Ms. Angela on her children's progress with StoryMaking. The children had been introduced to all StoryMaking Makerspaces, such as blocks, collage, and housekeeping, with the new purpose of playing with these materials to imagine a story. Launching the new purpose was the most important step in establishing a StoryMaking culture. After the focus lesson, each child was able to tell Ms. Angela where they were going, but not necessarily what story they were going to make that day. Off went Steven to blocks, where Ms. Angela watched him narrate his actions into a story!

One sunny day, the fish go in the house. *(Steven picks up the fish and places it inside his structure.)* And a bad wolf came. The fish run away. *(He makes the fish swim away.)* The bad wolf follow him. *(Steven picks up a yellow Lego and places it by the fish.)* He got away. He was sad about the bad wolf.

Steven continued to act out the fish and wolf chasing each other and described his actions for several more minutes as he explored the materials and began to imagine and make his story. Then Steven put all his materials back in their places and promptly left the blocks Makerspace. He headed to the collage Makerspace, and Ms. Angela was curious to see if he was going to tinker with a new story or remake the one he discovered when playing in blocks. He pulled out a piece of green felt to serve as his storyboard, began to pull items from collage, and then brought some materials he was playing with in blocks to remake his story. As Steven began to play and make, Ms. Angela sat down to inquire about his StoryMaking plan.

Steven explores materials in the blocks Makerspace to imagine, play, and make his story.

MS. ANGELA: What are you making, Steven?

STEVEN: I'm going to make my fish story.

Steven places his fish toy on the green felt. Ms. Angela quickly goes to her computer to upload the picture she had taken while he was playing with his blocks and prints it out for Steven to help him imagine the details he had just created in blocks. Steven begins to make.

STEVEN: One sunny day, the fish went in his house and the door was open. The bad wolf came. The fish ran away. The bad wolf followed him.

MS. ANGELA: Look at the story that you made in blocks. (*Ms. Angela points to the photo documentation.*) And then what happened?

Steven selects a scene from a magazine and a few buttons and places them on his green felt to make a pond.

STEVEN: The fish jumped in the pond.

MS. ANGELA: You made a pond, Steven. What a good detail! And then . . . ?

STEVEN: He got away!

MS. ANGELA: Is that the end?

STEVEN: I need some more things. (*Steven places a few more shiny jewels and some moss to represent the pond in his story. Then he moves the fish toward his pond, looks up, and smiles.*) The fish was glad! That's the end of my story!

Steven investigates his story and remakes it with collage materials.

Steven decided to remake his story and investigate how to revise and change the parts to create the story he wanted to share. With each sentence Steven would grab the physical material or loose part to represent a detail in his story. The children had been exploring for almost forty-five minutes and their time was coming to an end. Ms. Angela asked Steven what his next steps were for his story, and he enthusiastically declared as he pointed to the meeting area, "I want to tell it there! Where we share!" Steven felt confident in his story, and he was ready to go public by sharing his story with others.

Steven sat down at the meeting area with all his gathered materials for the Maker's Talk. He had decided to share his story with the collage materials with the class. He began to tell his story:

> One sunny day the fish went in his house. The door was open. A bad wolf came. The fish ran away to the pond. The bad wolf followed him. He jumped in the pond. He got away. The bad wolf was sad.

In his Maker's Talk, Steven combined details that he first explored in blocks and then added during his collage investigation. He decided that some details did not make sense or that he didn't like them before he shared his story with others. This four-year-old had just gone through an amazing process of exploring, investigating, and sharing—a process of inquiry where he imagined the materials he wanted to play with that day and made a story to share! Steven sat up proudly. Steven knew he was an inventor and author. Steven knew he was a StoryMaker!

STORYMAKING REQUIRES A CULTURE OF INQUIRY

Ann Pelo cautions that in a culture of inquiry, it is important to stay present in what children are currently wondering and curious about, so as educators we do not plan too far in advance. She explains: "Curriculum anchored in inquiry grows moment by moment, one step at a time, with the authentic participation of everyone in the community. This is invigorating work for teachers, and calls us to be critical and creative thinkers. To do this work we need to strengthen our skills in observation, reflection, and planning, and in the use of art media to represent ideas and emotion" (2017, 109).

The greatest distinction in inquiry teaching is how the class works together in a community to develop and use tools in the pursuit of new insights. In order to develop a culture of inquiry, teachers must develop a classroom community "that is underpinned by shared purposes and values; there are shared classroom routines and approaches; there are shared ways of talking that support the main purposes; the students have varied and changing roles and relationships" (Davidson 2009, 27).

When we introduce StoryMaking with our students, our first goal is to clearly express and explain how we will work together as we explore and tinker with our materials and in our Makerspaces each day. We show students the purpose of playing with the materials so they can explore and inquire into what stories they can discover and make. They know the purpose of using these materials, and we express the belief that the stories they make are valued by all in the classroom by providing time to share and by highlighting their work through displayed documentation to inspire others. Children learn ways to give compliments and advice during the share portion of StoryMaking. That builds a common routine as well as a purpose for talking with each other about their stories.

RITUALS AND ROUTINES FOR BUILDING A CULTURE OF STORYMAKING

The rituals and routines we outline for StoryMaking create a learning community in which children know what to expect and delight in the process of wondering and imagining their stories as they play. When children understand the purpose of their play and educators are there to facilitate their curiosities, children can reach their highest potential of learning.

Use Inquiry Routines with Children

Here are a few ways to build a culture of StoryMaking using inquiry with your children:

Cassandra is inspired by new materials placed in the collage Makerspace.

- Show your own curiosity with an inquiry mystery bag. Slowly reveal new materials from a bag during a focus lesson, circle time to start the day, or closing circle at the end of the day to prompt StoryMaking ideas before they go home. Model for children your own thoughts and wonderings and question the materials by saying, "What is this?" "What could I use this for in a story?" "What story could I make with this material?"

- Display new materials every two to three weeks to spark curiosity in a Makerspace. Ask children, "What stories can you imagine by looking at and touching these materials?" "What could you make?"

- Use thinking routines to teach children how to explore and wonder about tools and materials. A popular routine we use with our early learners is See, Think, Wonder (STW) (Ritchhart, Church, and Morrison 2011). Instead of telling them all about a tool, material, or new mentor text, engage the children in the STW routine below that we have adapted for StoryMaking. You could make this a weekly routine by establishing a Wondering Wednesday!

– See: "What do you see?" Provide children time to closely observe and touch the materials. Even provide magnifying lenses for them to explore the details closely.

– Think: "What things could we imagine making?"

– Wonder: "What stories does this make you wonder about making?"

• Establish a Wonder of the Week in your learning environment. In *A Place for Wonder*, Georgia Heard and Jennifer McDonough encourage us "to create a 'wonder world' that will help encourage children's curiosity and exploration" (2009, 10). We adapted their Wonder of the Week idea to encourage inquiry during StoryMaking. When you gather together at the start of the week, introduce the new wonder of the week. Hang a chart with a picture of a tool, material, or page from a book (or the actual artifact) to inspire children's wondering. Capture children's responses by writing their thinking below the question. As children try out their ideas, post documentation of their stories to inspire others.

This "Wonder of the Week" anchor chart shows sample questions and artifacts you can display to provoke the children's imaginations into making stories.

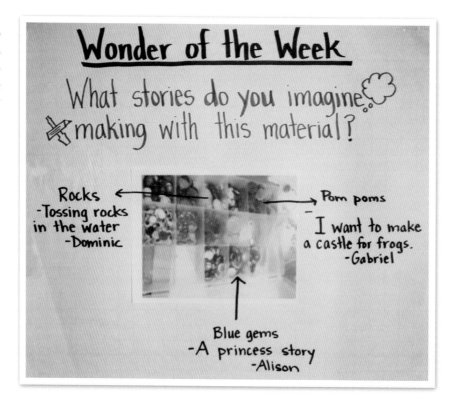

Wonder of the Week Chart Ideas

	Tool	Material	Mentor Text
Possible artifacts to display	Golf tees, string, raffia, tie wraps, low-temperature glue gun, screwdriver	Fabric squares, wood pieces, sand trays, squishy circuits, any loose parts	Picture of a character from a book, setting illustration, cover
Sample wonder questions for the week	How can you use this tool? What could you make? What stories do you imagine making with this tool?	How can you use this material? What could you make? What stories do you imagine making with this material?	How can you use this image to inspire a story? What character could you make? What places do you imagine for a story? How could you make a story like this author?

Imagine Stories throughout the Day

Another way to grow a culture of StoryMaking is to move toward a celebratory environment, where you model to children how stories can be discovered everywhere, all through the day, across disciplines and events, using whatever tools and materials and spaces and times are available and accessible. Below are some practical suggestions for how you can grow your rituals for StoryMaking throughout your day:

Morning meeting

- Begin the day by creating a story from the day before. For example, you could share about something that happened on the playground, during lunch, or at dismissal time. Provide a few props such as blocks to represent the event and equipment or people figures to help students visualize it.

- Give students time to turn and tell each other stories while others finish their morning routines and get settled into the day. Place students' StoryMaker folders in the center of their tables so they can locate a picture, illustration, or other form of documentation to select the story they want to share.

- Display a picture of a real event that happened to the class. Have the children make or share a story about that image by using the elements in the picture to explain key details, dialogue, feelings, and actions related to a story.

StoryMaking

- Begin the focus lesson by having a student share a story he made. It is very effective to show a video of a student sharing a story with his materials. This helps our youngest learners recall the story while their peers can visualize the parts of the story.

- Have a mid-workshop interruption to highlight a student's story. During the playing and making part of your workshop, stop the work to share a story one student created.

- End the workshop by making a story together about a real event.

- Alternately, end the workshop by sharing a student's story that had a beginning, and ask for advice on what else she could include in her story. This is a good strategy for students who keep playing without actually making a completed story. Have them bring their materials, and the class can work on a story for that child to continue and change the next day.

Transitions

- Have a sign-up sheet for students who want to share a story, and use this time to allow the students to share.

- Tell a short story after lunch or recess using something you noticed happening earlier in the day. This could be as simple as retelling what you said when the students went through the lunch line.

Closing circle/end of the day

- Look at the daily schedule posted and tell a story from one part of the day.

- Display a picture or other form of documentation from the day and have the children tell a story about it.

Anytime

- Have a chart in your classroom that displays StoryMaking ideas. Students can add their own pictures and ideas to this chart.

Model StoryMaking for Children

Modeling your own StoryMaking throughout the day is a critical component to creating routines and rituals for a culture of StoryMaking. During your focus lessons, you can introduce your family and hobbies as you make your stories. Modeling the StoryMaking process might be intimidating to some of us at first, but here are a few tips to help you get started as you grow your culture of StoryMaking:

Choose a real event that the class experienced. Our settings with young children are packed with stories just waiting to be told. You just have to be aware that the little details in your day can be woven into surprising and suspenseful stories that seem magical and interesting to the children. Observing children playing at the water table and splashing a little too rambunctiously can set the stage for a story filled with dialogue, feelings, and characters' actions. What seems like a common, everyday event can be turned into a silly story in which the students delight as they add dialogue and next events. You could use blocks or other materials to make a story about the water table, modeling StoryMaking. As these events happen throughout the day, it may be helpful to jot them on an anchor chart entitled "StoryMaker Ideas" or to write them on a sticky note to use later in your day.

Provide a beginning to set the scene. You can help get the story started with your students by providing them with the first line. If the class has had focus lessons on ways to begin a story, then you can offer them a choice. For example, use familiar opening phrases found in favorite books, such as "One day . . ." and "Once upon a time . . . ," and show them the book's first page. Collage offers a perfect backdrop for setting the scene, as you can use a piece of felt or material, a placemat, a scrapbook background, or a photograph as your setting (background). The students can add parts as you make the story together.

If the students have not yet had a focus lesson on ways to begin a story, then this is a perfect opportunity to frontload or model skills that they will be explicitly taught later in a StoryMaker lesson. We will provide more specific lessons on ways to begin a story in chapters 4 through 6.

Share a story sequentially. Have you ever walked into your favorite department store without a list and suddenly have a cart full of items you don't really need? We have, and the same kind of situation can happen when you launch into a story without a plan for how it will go or a list of ingredients that you need. One of the best strategies we have taught our early learners is how to imagine before they play (or make) their stories. Creating an anchor chart that lists a menu of options along with picture cues helps students pick who their story is about (the characters), where their story takes places (the setting), and what happens (events or actions). We discuss how to create these anchor charts in chapter 5.

Children involved in StoryMaking for five months were able to imagine stories everywhere. They created this story based on their shared experience of taking walks outside to notice buildings and structures.

We have provided some ideas about how you can engage children in Story-Making through inquiry each day. We've also demonstrated how you can model StoryMaking throughout the day. The results of your hard work will become evident quickly, as there are many benefits for children. The main learning outcomes documented in the research of the maker movement are increased agency and character. We have seen evidence of both of these attributes in our young StoryMakers.

A STORYMAKING CULTURE BUILDS AGENCY AND CHARACTER

In a StoryMaking culture, there are shared values, routines, and rituals within a community of learners. StoryMakers come to know that they each have unique stories that will be valued and honored. They will learn common routines, like gathering for focus lessons, playing with fun materials, and sharing their stories with one another. And there are engaging rituals, like building stories of an event that happened during the day. But growing a StoryMaking culture goes beyond routines and rituals. The maker's mind-set includes positive qualities we hope to cultivate in children. A mind-set is "a way of seeing and being in the world" (Clapp et al. 2017, 87). Educators involved in the maker movement have found that the primary learning outcomes of making are development of agency and character. A StoryMaking culture attends to both. Simply put, agency is an I-can-do-it approach. Clapp and colleagues define it as "feeling empowered to make choices about how to act in the world" (19). Character involves "self making . . . , building competence, building confidence, and forming identities" (25–26).

> **• Voices from the Field •**
>
> "I think it [StoryMaking culture] is respecting their thinking. It's not pushing their structures off as unimportant. It's really valuing the child as a learner. . . . That's the culture that's different in my classroom. I see each one of them as capable and functioning members of our classroom society, and therefore they see themselves as capable functioning members. . . . It's constantly respecting. Giving them the respect of thinking that they're capable. And the space and time. It does take a lot of time to get them from the idea to the end piece."
>
> —Rachel, integrated pre-K teacher

Lots of opportunities to build a sense of agency are accessible in a StoryMaking culture. Children are invited to play, make, and grow stories individually and with friends. Initially provocations, or invitations (materials, tools, experiences, lessons), provide avenues for children to follow their interests, gain fluency with uses of tools and materials, and get to know themselves, others, and their worlds better. Providing choices is a first step toward developing a can-do attitude, as children select their spaces, materials, tools, and friends during Story-Making. Because students are encouraged to select materials of their choice to create the stories of their choice and present them in languages of their choice, Story-Making creates an inclusive community that celebrates each story while building the agency of our young learners.

A culture of StoryMaking also provides opportunities for self-making, or building character, as the children make the stories of their everyday worlds. As they engage regularly in StoryMaking, practicing with tools and materials and making their stories, children acquire confidence and increase competence. Children gain self-efficacy when they learn that their stories matter, they are the authors of their stories, and they have unique stories to share.

The children come to know that they will have many opportunities to persevere, overcome barriers, and try again. They learn to take risks and try new things during StoryMaking because they know they will still be considered part of the community, even if they fail or get frustrated. As they become experts and innovators in the uses of materials and in StoryMaking, our young children build character.

STORYMAKING BEHAVIORS

Now that you have been flooding your classroom with rituals that encourage curiosity and build agency and character, you'll want to know whether your efforts are working. We have combined the work of John Barell (2013), who identified behaviors that curious people display, and Lisa Regalla (2016), who named characteristics of a maker's mind-set, to create a list of what you may see and hear as you develop your own StoryMaking culture. These behaviors are listed below, with specific examples we have observed when children are exploring and making their stories. When you begin to see and hear these behaviors, it means a StoryMaking culture has been established.

StoryMakers wonder. They exhibit curiosity when they play with new materials, explore new spaces, and investigate their worlds while they make the stories of their everyday lives. When new materials are presented to the children for StoryMaking, they notice. They may think the materials are strange or fascinating and exclaim to their friends, "Whoa, look at this!" or "What story can I make with this?"

StoryMakers observe. Children spend time feeling and looking closely at new materials, but they examine these materials even more closely when they return to them to tinker with a story. For example, when a child was using collage materials to create a scene for her rainy-day story, she carefully studied the texture of the jewels, buttons, and other loose parts. She initially placed a feather down to represent water but went back to study the shiny jewels. She examined the texture of each material to determine which one better represented the water in the story. She selected the jewels because the shiny texture reminded her of the water. We see children examine shape, texture, size, and color when they tinker and make their stories.

As Roland tinkers with his story, he considers his choices of materials.

StoryMakers explore. With the teacher as facilitator, children are guided through exploring and inquiring about the materials presented to them for the purpose of imagining a story. The child's first role is to explore and inquire into the materials. The initial wondering about and engagement with the materials open up entry points for deep exploration. We typically see children explore in two ways. They may return to the same material to remake a story that sparked their interest, repurposing the materials to change details. Or they may return to the same story but instead use a different material to explore new details.

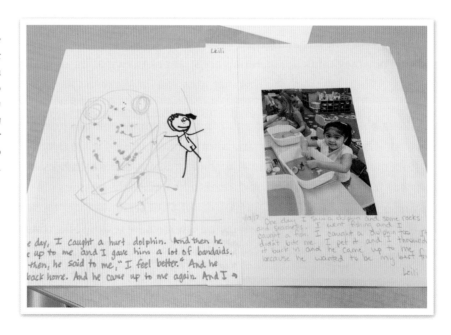

Leili first made her story with art materials. Then she returned to her imagined story the following day and used water tub materials to remake it.

StoryMakers innovate. Lisa Regalla explains that many of our great thinkers were both innovators *and* artists. For example, Einstein was a physicist *and* musician. Each of our spaces can become Makerspaces during StoryMaking. Children can make stories in the tinkering studio *and* in housekeeping, in blocks *and* in collage. As a child returns to materials or story ideas, their role changes from an explorer and inquirer to a tinkerer and investigator. When children choose different Makerspaces or materials to explore and make their story, they are asking themselves, "What if I try clay today?" "How will that material help me imagine a story?"

StoryMakers persist. Stamina and persistence are built over time and take lots of practice!

When the children leave the meeting area after our focus lesson, they often are able to explain what Makerspace or materials they want to work with but are unsure of what story they will make. But the children continue to play, using different materials that eventually spark a memory or idea. They call out with great pride and excitement, "I am making my story!" rather than give up. With repeated use of the inquiry framework for teaching, children learn to consider new possibilities and different angles to their stories. They stay with the same story and remake a version by using a variety of materials to see if there is more of the story they want to share.

StoryMakers collaborate. During StoryMaking, children learn to seek advice and opinions not only during share time but also while they make their stories. When they think they are done with their story, the children of course want to share it with you so you can take a picture and document the story. You can't see every student at once, however, and you want to avoid the mad rush of children wanting to tell their stories when you are working with another child. It's therefore important to model lessons on how children can use one another as resources. They can tell their story to their friends. The other children can learn to ask questions, such as pointing to the picture and saying, "What is this part?" They also can learn to give advice on ways to consider adding or changing a detail in the story. Children become interested in what their peers think and feel, and they in turn want to contribute to helping their friends make their story.

StoryMakers reflect. At the end of each unit of study and during the final phase of the inquiry framework, it is important to prompt children to view their documentation and reflect on all they have learned. Teachers capture photo documentation, illustrations, and children's dictation of their story versions so children can choose to publish in a "book." This documentation allows the children to observe their process and explain what they learned about making stories.

Children share their stories and seek advice from one another.

StoryMakers enact a growth mind-set. Regalla states, "A growth mind-set promotes the belief that capabilities can be continuously developed, improved, and refined through experiences that involve success, mistakes, and persistence" (2016, 267). One way she suggests building a growth mindset is by offering "process" praise—praise related to what children do rather than who they are. That's easy with our young learners as they are always doing! We've heard teachers say, "I see that you're really working hard on your collage. I can't wait for you to share your story!" or "I noticed that you shared your blocks with others when you were making your story. Thank you for being a good friend."

When educators implement an inquiry framework to help plan instruction and begin to see and hear the behaviors described above, the culture of StoryMaking is well on its way to becoming established and will continue to grow and flourish one step at a time. Next we describe the inquiry phases within our framework and show how each of the phases looks and sounds during StoryMaking.

THE THREE PHASES OF INQUIRY

There are many inquiry frameworks to choose from, and it is important to realize that there is not one correct framework. Educators should examine the frameworks available and choose one that they find best reflects their beliefs about learning and works for the level and age of their students. When we began the journey of implementing an inquiry-based curriculum, a group of our teachers and specialists examined many cycles, including those of John Dewey, Kath Murdoch, Kathy Short, and Barbara Stripling; the 5 E's and the Big 6 Skills; the inquiry approach descriptions from Stephanie Harvey and Harvey Daniels; and the phases of project work from Lilian Katz, just to name a few. We highlighted important parts from each framework but found that some of them included too many phases or steps for our earliest learners to use.

One of the hurdles we noticed was that young children could often move through our StoryMaker Cycle in a matter of minutes or in a day as they constructed new meaning while StoryMaking. Since children are constantly choosing play-based centers, they flow from one Makerspace to another. This movement means that the children as a group are always at different places in the StoryMaking process at different times. It seemed too difficult to manage the many phases of some frameworks. We needed a framework that allowed for this continual movement. Narrowing our framework to three phases also made it manageable for our teachers to document and record what phase of the inquiry framework the children were in during their process of StoryMaking.

Below is a description of our inquiry framework (a framework from which teachers could plan instruction according to students' needs and curiosities) and what each phase means in the StoryMaking process. The behaviors described are based on observational data gathered from all the teachers who created a StoryMaking experience and from the research of learning practices observed when children are in the process of making.

Phase 1: Explore

The purpose of Phase 1, "Explore," for StoryMaking is for students to fully explore all the materials and tools to help them imagine stories to make. Children approach the materials with great excitement and curiosity. At this point, our learners are more focused on the properties of the materials rather than on how the materials can help them make a story. Provide large amounts of time for children to question and fully explore these materials without preconceived outcomes in the beginning. They will want to use all their senses to explore and question the shape, size, texture, and color of each treasure they encounter. You might also observe your earliest learners wondering about sound and weight as they dump and fill containers with found materials or loose parts. This is a normal progression of how children question and explore before they settle in and use the materials for a purpose. When providing children new art materials, Ann Pelo (2017) explains that children must first begin with art explorations. Then she slowly invites children to explore ways in which they can use the art medium for representation. The same is true for the maker's tools and materials. This is called the tinkering phase. Eventually children will begin to imagine how they can use their materials for StoryMaking and tinker with the materials and tools provided.

Joel explores his materials to begin to imagine a story.

During this time, teachers model ways to imagine, play, and make a story using a variety of materials (blocks, clay, weaving, woodworking, water table, paint) during focus lessons. They observe and document the discovery process, recording each type of material the children are using and capturing photos and children's dictation of each story idea they have made. It is important to provide lessons that use mentor texts to build children's vocabulary (words about feelings, describing words, sensory words) so children develop language to tell the stories they have made.

Even though we proceed to Phase 2 in our instruction to model the next step of the framework, children may act in a different way. Early learners especially may decide after playing and making their story with one set of materials that it is perfect, they are all done, and they want to share. This is perfectly normal and should be celebrated. With consistent modeling during focus lessons, however, even the earliest learners will learn to investigate and try their story with different materials.

When students have developed fluency for playing and making a variety of stories and begin using the language and vocabulary to tell their stories, it's time to move into Phase 2. You may hear children saying, "I made my story!" informing you that they understand the purpose of StoryMaking. Another indication that they understand is when they begin to use the vocabulary you have taught them, such as feeling words, in their StoryMaking

Phase 1 Elements and Student and Teacher Processes

Elements of the child's inquiry process	What students are doing in the inquiry process	What teachers are doing in the inquiry process
Initial Engagement • Lessons help invite curiosity, build background knowledge, imagine topics/stories, and instill wonder. • Materials, objects, events, or questions, are used to provoke and imagine use of materials and/or stories. • Data is gathered to determine what children already know and what they can do. **Exploring and Inquiring** • Materials, tools, and ideas are explored. • Hands-on activities are used, with guidance and support.	**Imagine:** Freely explore the materials and tools with all senses to imagine new uses. **Play:** Play and tinker with materials and tools to become inspired. **Make:** Ask questions and make predictions about how children can use the materials and tools. **Share:** Demonstrate materials children chose and used during making.	**Imagine:** Model imagining story ideas and a curious approach through exploration of materials and tools. **Play:** Model purposeful play and tinkering with materials and tools. Create Makerspaces and new purposes for play. **Make:** Facilitate small-group formation to ensure heterogeneous groups with compatible interests to share resources. Confer with small groups and individuals to support making. **Share:** Share your own curiosity and making process. Use documentation tools to capture patterns of how children use materials and story ideas. Share documentation with children.

Phase 2: Investigate

During Phase 2, "Investigate," children are encouraged to return to a story and remake it using a different material or the same materials. The purpose of this phase is for children to try different versions of their stories (revising) by repurposing materials they have already used to represent an added or changed detail in the story. By revisiting materials they have used previously, they begin to modify, enhance, or create new elements or parts of their story. Peter Wardrip and Lisa Brahms (2015) describe this process as "hack and repurpose." At the Children's Museum of Pittsburgh's MAKESHOP, they witnessed the behaviors of learners disassociating the properties of an object from its most familiar use. They discovered that learners use everyday materials in useful or new ways. Similarly in StoryMaking, children no longer see the object as a button from a jacket but maybe as the center of their bright sun. And if they used that object as their sun in the first version of the story, they may refine the use of the small buttons during Phase 2 and discover that this material would work better representing the ants crawling on the ground.

Teachers in this phase seek out resources such as strong mentor texts to share with children about how authors and illustrators start their stories and create details in their settings and other story elements. These ongoing demonstrations give children strategies for purposeful play. Teachers also facilitate children sharing with each other for the purpose of seeking advice. Children develop an interest in the opinions and feelings of their peers and ultimately seek their attention. At the beginning they may shout to their friends sitting next to them in the collage Makerspace, "Hey, look what I made!" With each return through the StoryMaker Cycle, however, children learn other ways to use one another. They learn that they can ask their peers a question such as "How did you make that?" to seek advice that will enhance their story or their fluency in using a specific material.

Interest may decline during this phase, and children may choose to return to imagining new ways to use a material or tool or be inspired with a new story idea that may lead them back to Phase 1. Educators can introduce new materials or set up provocation areas to re-engage the learners and help children investigate the best version of their stories.

When children have had the opportunity to investigate the best version of their story and to remake it using a variety of materials, teachers guide them through the final phase of going public.

Phase 2 Elements and Student and Teacher Processes

Elements of the child's inquiry process	What students are doing in the inquiry process	What teachers are doing in the inquiry process
Investigating • Students learn to develop questions, search for information, and discover answers and new details. • New concepts, skills, and materials are introduced to support investigation. • Materials and situations allow students to build on or extend understanding and skill.	**Imagine:** Express the intention of a story idea to pursue or materials to use. Ask and answer questions, think of new ideas. **Play:** Hack and take apart materials to discover the best purpose for the children's story. Repurpose materials, tools, and processes to modify, enhance, or create a new story. **Make:** Use strategies for making meaning and seek out a variety of resources to remake stories. Build with increasing fluency using a variety of tools, materials, and processes. **Share:** Use materials and tools to share stories.	**Imagine:** Model how to imagine materials or story ideas with a question in mind. **Play:** Flood children with resources and materials on an idea, topic, or question. **Make:** Help students sharpen or change materials or story ideas. Model use of materials and tools in new or more complex ways while conferring with groups and individuals. **Share:** Use documentation tools to capture developing and changing products and processes to share with children.

Phase 3: Communicate

During Phase 3, "Communicate," children have a variety of options for sharing their story with others. The purpose of this phase is to share what they have made with an audience, reflect on new learning, and celebrate their accomplishments as a StoryMaker. Sharing may be in the form of a published book, but not necessarily. Children may choose to sign up for a Maker's Talk to tell, act out, or display their story. Teachers provide a variety of ways for children to express their story and all they have learned as StoryMakers. Loris Malaguzzi, founder of the Reggio Emilia approach, expresses beautifully that children have "a hundred ways of thinking of playing, of speaking" (1998, 3). Therefore we want to expand the concept of publishing to include the many "languages" our children possess. For specific examples of how children can share their learning, see chapter 6.

Phase 3 Elements and Student and Teacher Processes

Elements of the child's inquiry process	What students are doing in the inquiry process	What teachers are doing in the inquiry process
Communicating • Children share learning, demonstrate understanding, and go public. • Children reflect on their new knowledge, skills, and abilities.	**Imagine:** Choose a way to publish or go public based on the topic and audience. **Play:** Ask new questions about materials or story ideas. **Make:** Revise and improve the chosen piece to share. Set new goals for making. **Share:** Reflect on the process using their own products (published stories).	**Imagine:** Co-construct expectations for final pieces. **Play:** Provide choices for students to share/perform their stories. **Make:** Support children in finding real audiences and opportunities to share their stories. **Share:** Facilitate children reflecting on content and process. Display documentation for reflection and celebration.

INCLUDING FAMILIES IN THE STORYMAKING CULTURE

Family members are an integral part of a StoryMaking culture. As you begin to develop a StoryMaking culture in your classroom, be sure to include families in the process. Below are ways families can take part in your StoryMaking community:

- Family members are honored and welcomed. Initially families are getting to know the expectations, routines, and rules of your spaces and materials. They can learn about StoryMaking from notes you send home and from pictures of their children engaged in StoryMaking, accompanied by their children's words. Families love to see evidence of their children engaged and learning. StoryMaking offers a perfect opportunity for picture taking and dictation, and for posting evidence of learning on the walls and bulletin boards and on apps. Invite the families into your StoryMaking culture this way.

- Families understand StoryMaking's purpose. The families become familiar with routines and expectations. They begin to identify their children as StoryMakers as they observe them imagining, playing, and making. They may encourage their children to share their stories and start to ask their children "What stories did you make today?"

- Families become StoryMakers. This is when the families start to imagine, play, and make stories with their children at home in the evenings and on weekends. They know that any event is a possible setting for a story, like filling up the gas tank or taking a trip to the store. Encourage them to bring in stories that they make with their children. They are part of the StoryMaking community!

FINAL THOUGHTS

In a StoryMaking culture, all children belong as each child has unique stories to imagine, play, make, and share. We have explored the rituals and routines that lead to the formation of an inclusive community. When children are tinkering with materials in the collage Makerspace, they are learning through inquiry. They are uncovering and making the stories of their lives to communicate with others. They are learning about agency and character. They are building the everyday stories of their lives within a culture of StoryMaking.

Children demonstrate the actions of StoryMakers in a StoryMaking culture: they wonder, observe, explore, innovate, persist, collaborate, reflect, and enact a growth mind-set. This of course does not happen on its own. It occurs when the teacher is intentional in providing opportunities for children to develop agency and character. In a StoryMaking culture, the children are empowered to make choices as they enter the explore phase of inquiry. During Phases 2 and 3, children build character as they gain confidence in their abilities and identify themselves as Story-Makers. Educators wonder, play, and make stories in front of and alongside their children as a community of learners, inquirers, and StoryMakers. This partnership will unleash the creativity and imagination inside each child to play, make, and share stories about their own world!

TIPS FOR STUDENTS WITH SPECIAL RIGHTS

- Model your own curiosity and problem-solving skills using materials and tools. Children often ask questions but look to us for answers. Become a Play & Make partner with a student and discover how to use a material together. Say "I don't know, let's find out together." Engage in free exploration and model ways to play using materials so they can discover and replicate its many uses. For example, model ways to stack blocks to build a road, use figurines to act out a conversation, or use tie wraps to hold materials together.

- If a child is not yet ready to make a story, then they can share their maker's mind-set by showing how to use a particular material or demonstrate an innovative use of a tool during a Maker's Talk. A StoryMaking culture is an inclusive community where everyone's imagination and skills are valued and honored.

Maker's Moment

Conner imagined using the puppets during StoryMaking. He selected the gorilla and began acting out a story. When Michelle checked in with him after observing his action for several minutes, Conner told her the story he was in the process of making:

Connor shares his first version of his story using a puppet.

(continued)

"One day, I went to the zoo. I saw a gorilla. He stood up and did this." (He pounds chest.)

Conner continued to play and make his story. After about forty minutes, the children began cleaning up, and he wanted to share his story:

"Gorilla grew big and strong. (He added actions during his retell—and a truck.) One time, there was a little gorilla and then he was growing bigger and bigger and bigger. And then he came a big gorilla. (Conner acted out the gorilla smashing the truck.) And then he smashed the whole world!"

The following week Conner wanted to continue to make his gorilla story. This time he imagined using the Legos to help him investigate his story details.

Conner shares his remade story.

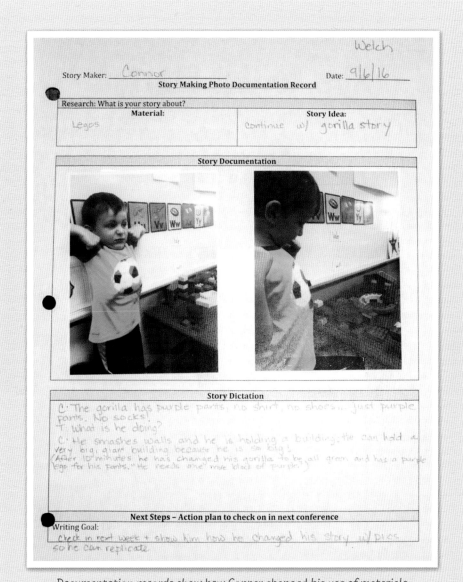

Story Maker: Connor   Welch   Date: 9/6/16

Story Making Photo Documentation Record

Research: What is your story about?

Material:	Story Idea:
Legos	continue w/ gorilla story

Story Documentation

Story Dictation

C: The gorilla has purple pants, no shirt, no shoes... just purple pants. No socks!
T: What is he doing?
C: He smashes walls and he is holding a building. He can hold a very big, giant building because he is so big.
(After 10 minutes he has changed his gorilla to be all green and has a purple lego for his pants. "He needs one more block of purple.")

Next Steps – Action plan to check on in next conference

Writing Goal:
Check in next week + show him how he changed his story w/ pics so he can replicate

Documentation records show how Conner changed his use of materials to more accurately represent the character he imagined.

CONNER: The gorilla has purple pants, no shirt, and no shoes. Just purple pants. No socks!

MICHELLE: What is he doing?

CONNER: He smashes walls and he is holding a building. He can hold a very big, giant building because he is so big!

Conner continued to investigate his story for another ten minutes. He started to repurpose how he was using the materials to represent his character. He changed his gorilla to be all green and used a purple Lego for his pants. Conner said confidently, "He just needs one more block of purple."

CHAPTER 4

How to Get Started

A FIRST LESSON IN STORYMAKING

One Monday morning early in the school year, Michelle gathered on the carpet with an eager group of pre-K students ready to play in Ms. Rachel's class housed at our local museum. She introduced this new time of day as StoryMaking by greeting the children as StoryMakers.

MICHELLE: Good morning, StoryMakers!

CLASS: Good morning!

MICHELLE: Did you hear what I called you?

CLASS: Yeah!

MICHELLE: What did I call you?

CLASS: StoryMakers!

MICHELLE: That's right! Today, we are going to learn how StoryMakers work to make stories. When we come to the meeting area, we are first going to have a lesson. And then, guess what's next?

CLASS: What? (*In squealy, excited voices.*)

MICHELLE: We get to go off and imagine, play, and make our stories! Then the last part is that we are going to come back and share. (*She points around the circle to show each part.*)

SEVERAL STUDENTS SHOUT: I want to share!

MICHELLE: The first thing we do is have a lesson. (*Michelle picks up a picture of the class sitting on the carpet listening to the teacher and tapes it to that section of the chart.*) Let's talk about what happens in the lesson. Study the picture. What is the teacher doing in the picture?

SARAYIAH: Talking.

MICHELLE: That's right! (*Michelle labels the picture with a sticky note explaining the actions of the teacher.*) Now what are the students supposed to be doing in a lesson?

SEVERAL STUDENTS: Listening ears!

MICHELLE: (*Michelle labels the picture.*) So let's have our lesson. Did you know that when you play with materials like blocks or Legos, you can also imagine a story? So I'm going to play in front of you, and I'm going to see if it helps me imagine a story to share.

Michelle reached for several wooden blocks and began building in front of the students. This was the beginning of the year, and the students had been working on their portraits, so she took several blocks and began to build her face. She told the students that she was playing to see if that would help her imagine a story. Michelle reached for the Legos to find smaller pieces for her portrait and placed them down on the carpet for her eyes and nose. Michelle then stopped and explained to the students that she was imagining an idea.

Children learn the StoryMaking routine by interacting with an anchor chart.

Michelle models the StoryMaking routine during a focus lesson.

Michelle said, "You know what, StoryMakers? When I placed the Legos down for my eyes to create my face, it made me think of something I saw with my eyes this weekend. Do you know what I saw? I was looking out the window and I saw lots of trees out the window."

She grabbed a few cylinder blocks and built several trees in front of the students. She continued to explain that she had seen a red bird and placed a red Lego on top of the structure. Just then she dramatically exclaimed, "Oh my goodness, I imagined a story I can make!" She continued to explain the process that she was playing with her materials when she imagined an idea. She continued to play and finished making her story idea. Now she was ready to share her story.

Through this very first focus lesson, Michelle unraveled the mystery of how we should begin when we want to try StoryMaking with our children. She modeled the

StoryMaker Cycle and suggested a new purpose when playing with our materials, the purpose of imagining the stories in our lives. In this chapter, we will provide you with step-by-step lessons for your first StoryMaking unit on how to get started and a sequence of instruction for Phase 1, "Explore," where the purpose is for children to fully explore all the materials and tools to help them imagine stories to make.

HOW PLAY LEADS TO STORYMAKING

Our StoryMaking cycle starts with igniting a child's imagination, and play can provide time and space for young children to begin to use their imaginations. Matt Glover highlights the importance of play in his work that "according to Vygotsky (1966), pretend play is the leading activity of the preschool and kindergarten period because it leads to developmental accomplishments, such as imagination, higher levels of thinking (for example, problem solving), and self-regulation" (Glover 2009, 71). Glover explains that children's dramatic play connects storytelling and writing naturally: "It is not uncommon for children to tell stories based on pictures they draw. Children will draw or paint a picture and then tell an elaborate story about their picture" (72). We have observed children becoming inspired to play and make a story with any material in any area when they are provided with a new purpose to explore, a purpose of making stories. That is why we have created the first set of lessons to introduce a wide variety of Makerspaces and materials for your children to explore and imagine a story to play and make. The main purpose of the focus lessons is not to impose academic skills onto our earliest learners that they may not be ready for; it is to model our thinking in a StoryMaking culture. When we become a StoryMaker alongside our children during a focus lesson, they become inspired to go off and play and make their own stories. Children do learn academic skills along the way, of course, but we want to make it very clear that their play and making are at the heart of the StoryMaking experience.

The StoryMaker Cycle includes a focus lesson to explore a new strategy or material, a time to imagine new possibilities with their materials, independent time to play and make, and finally a time to share. We like to describe this cycle as "controlled chaos." It is messy and at times disorderly, which is the nature of inquiry-based learning. Mike McGalliard explains similar behaviors in his Creative Play Spiral, a maker model that begins with the children's inspiration and culminates with the sharing of the actual artifact built. He writes that "it may not be until a child 'plays' with available materials that they get 'inspired' to make something" (2016, 117). A child may also repeat components of the cycle many times throughout Phases 1, 2, and 3 of our StoryMaking units. For example, a child may repeat the "play" and "make" part of the StoryMaker Cycle and "imagine" a new way to remake their story.

Focus Lessons and the Inquiry Framework

The lessons in chapters 4, 5, and 6 are designed to help you and your children progress through Phases 1, 2, and 3 of any StoryMaking unit. To help you understand this progression, the table below outlines the purpose of each phase's focus lessons and the objective of the lessons within each phase.

Focus Lesson Purpose and Objective

Focus Lesson Purpose	Lesson Objectives
Phase 1 "Explore" **Focus Lessons (chapter 4)** The purpose is for children to fully explore all the materials and tools to help them imagine stories to make.	• Children will understand the purpose of StoryMaking by creating a chart and living each part (presented in the first unit only or whenever needed to remind children of routine). • Children will share a story from their lives by using materials to make this moment. • Children will make a story by using materials in a new Makerspace (change materials throughout the year). • Children will learn how to come up with a story idea by discovering the ideas of real authors.
Phase 2 "Investigate" **Focus Lessons (chapter 5)** The purpose is for children to return to a story and remake it using a different material or to repurpose the same materials to create a better version of their story.	• Children will return to a story idea by choosing new materials to remake their story. • Children will organize their documentation by using their own StoryMaker folder (presented in the first unit only or whenever needed to remind children of routine). • Children will plan before they play by using an anchor chart to express intention. • Children will tell a story by using mentor texts to help them know how to start. • Children will add details to their illustrations by studying the work of other illustrators.
Phase 3 "Communicate" **Focus Lessons (chapter 6)** The purpose is for children to choose a way to share their story with others.	• Children will share a story by using one of the Hundred Languages referred to by Malaguzzi (e.g., song, dance, playdough). • Children will use documentation to help them write their story on paper. • Children will select a way to publish by studying the parts of a mentor text.

The Workshop Model

Our StoryMaking time of day follows a workshop model of instruction. We chose this model because it "can balance play and direct instruction, inquiry and scaffolded practice, creativity and choice, community and autonomy. It is a model that adapts to the very specific needs of the students" (Mraz and Hertz 2015, 11). The workshop approach has been widely used in reading and writing and is the foundation of the work of educators Donald Graves, Lucy Calkins, Katie Wood Ray, and many others. Below are the major parts of the model, including the focus lesson and the StoryMaker Cycle:

Focus Lesson. Each workshop begins with a focus lesson, which is how we also begin our StoryMaking time of day. The focus lesson for StoryMaking is a time when the teacher provides direct or inquiry instruction to focus on and explore the use of a material or tool, or even to become inspired by a story idea. Modeling the parts of each component is important; therefore you will notice each component in the focus lessons is described with suggested language for teaching.

Imagine. We provide a moment for children to pause and reflect on what they observed during the focus lesson. This is a time when teachers will support children in selecting a material or a Makerspace that they will use for making that day. Of course children may need time to play with materials before becoming inspired. Documentation forms will be important during this process so you can record the frequency and use of materials and story ideas.

Play & Make. Next the children leave the meeting area for independent work time. During StoryMaking this is when students play and make by choosing a specific Makerspace or material in the learning environment. The three components of Play & Make are discussed below.

Share. Share time is when children gather back together to share what they learned or the teacher uses this time to reinforce the learning. For StoryMaking, children gather to share the stories they made along with their materials and how they made their story. In our early learning environments, we encourage them to first give compliments and then, over time, thoughtful suggestions. We continue to grow our possibilities during our share time. The most common way to end our StoryMaking is by providing a special time called the "Maker's Talk," when a few children are selected or volunteer to share how they made their story with their friends. You can read more about ways to share in chapter 6.

Another common practice during share time is to practice collaborative storytelling. As described in chapter 3, storytelling can be a part of StoryMaking. When you choose a real event experienced by the class, use materials to make it with the children, and discuss each element of the event as you make it, you are using another wonderful way to share and create a powerful culture of story.

In *The Art of Teaching Reading*, Lucy Calkins (2001) describes a framework for teaching, which she calls her architecture of a mini-lesson. This structure has been extremely helpful for our teachers, and you will see the same components represented in the Focus & Explore portion of each lesson. Below are the components of the mini-lesson:

Bentley shares his story during a Maker's Talk.

Connect. Each lesson begins with a connection. This is an opportunity for the teacher to make a connection using a personal story or previous learning to support the lesson objective for that day.

Teach. The teaching component is the direct instruction portion of the lesson. You may also use inquiry-style teaching during this portion, where the educator poses a provocation or question for the children to discover the answer to together.

Active Involvement. The active involvement portion of the lesson allows children to try out what you have taught. Children often turn and talk to a partner to practice the new skill, independently plan and make a part of the story, or collaboratively work on the new skill together. The educator observes the students during this brief time to assess their current understanding. The purpose of the active involvement is to gauge the students' understanding of the focus lesson before sending them to do independent and collaborative work.

Don't worry if this teaching structure seems unfamiliar. We provide examples of a demonstration-style and an inquiry-style lesson later in this chapter.

GETTING STARTED IN STORYMAKING

Many teachers of early learners who we worked with wondered at the beginning, "How should I introduce this to my students?" and "What do the first lessons look like so I can prepare my students and myself?" Let us remind you that there is no one "right" way. You have choices! In our classrooms, we implemented four Story-Making units throughout the year, each unit approximately nine weeks long, with a connection to nature, colors, structures, and light, and corresponding materials. Should you want to implement these four units, we provide a year-long plan highlighting the focus lessons for each unit on the book's product page at www .redleafpress.org. We encourage you to substitute your own units, however, based on your needs and the interests of your children.

When you begin any new unit, you will be entering into Phase 1, "Explore," of your instruction, as described in chapter 3. The purpose of this phase is for children to fully explore all the materials to imagine their story. Since this is the very first time your children will be entering into an inquiry framework with StoryMaking, you will have to insert some management lessons so they know the purpose and routines of this new way to play. You will also have to guide all children through each step of the StoryMaker Cycle so they experience how StoryMakers work. In later units, students will go through the cycle at their own pace, but for now they still need to learn the steps on how to go from play to make to share. Let's take a look into the unit to see what we recommend for the initial lesson.

Introducing StoryMaking

It's important to clarify with the children the purpose of StoryMaking and what they will be expected to do each day. Modeling the parts of StoryMaking will make this part of their day clear. You will explain that "this time of day on our daily schedule is called StoryMaking. When we gather on the carpet at this time every day, we will always have a focus lesson and then go to Makerspaces to play for the purpose of making a story, and then we will come back to share and participate in a Maker's Talk." Make StoryMaking a part of the schedule and add a sign to the daily schedule. Create an anchor chart that includes photos and documentation to help show students what the parts look like. Make annotations on sticky notes labeling what you would like students to pay attention to in the photos. Continue to add documentation in the next few lessons as you model each material to the students as the next step. Add a pointer to the anchor chart to show children where you are in the process. This chart can eventually be retired after children know the routine.

First StoryMaking anchor chart

---------- STORYMAKING FOCUS LESSON ----------

Introduction

Objective: Children will understand the purpose of StoryMaking by creating a chart and living each part.

MATERIALS

- "StoryMakers Work Like This . . ." anchor chart drawn on a large piece of paper
- Sticky notes for annotation
- Marker
- One photo of the class in an area where you gather for teaching
- One photo of a child playing with a material to serve as example
- One photo of a child sharing in a special area in your teaching area (This photo could be staged prior to the lesson and used to explain "Share" during the focus lesson.)
- Camera to capture documentation

FOCUS & EXPLORE

Connect: *"We have been learning how to play in our areas, and now I would like to show you how we can play in a different way during StoryMaking."* Reference this time on the daily schedule posted. *"Every day at the start of StoryMaking, we will gather on the carpet for a lesson. Today we are all going to be StoryMakers, and I will show you what StoryMakers can do."* Show a picture of yourself teaching the class. Label the picture with expectations you have been reinforcing (listening ears, teacher talking). Add this annotated picture to the chart.

Teach: Show children how they can play with materials to inspire a story. Explain to them that now they will listen to the lesson. *"StoryMakers, every day we learn while playing in our areas. We get to play with blocks and housekeeping. These are called materials. I am going to play with my materials to see if they inspire a story to make."* Begin creating a scene or a portrait of yourself with a material, such as blocks. Provide think-alouds as you choose your materials and label what you are doing.

"StoryMakers, I was building a portrait of my face, and when I made my eyes with the Legos, it made me remember something that I saw." Continue to add to the story with materials to explain what you saw. *"Do you know what just happened, StoryMakers? I was playing with my materials and inspiration hit me! I made a story, and now I am ready to share my story!"* Tell a short story with a simple beginning, middle, and end. If this is too much for your students, just state a sentence. Don't be elaborate with too many details at the beginning because we want students to be able to replicate the process and to feel like they can do this too.

Refer to the chart and explain that that was the focus lesson. *"Every day we will learn a new way that will help us become better at making our stories."* Move the arrow to the "imagine, play, and make our stories" smiling face part of the anchor chart. *"Now, we have to get ready for the biggest part of our StoryMaking, where we get inspired by a story idea to play and make."* Show students a picture of themselves playing with a specific material, then label the material and place the annotated picture on the anchor chart. Continue to add documentation as you introduce each Makerspace or material throughout the next series of lessons.

"Then after we are done playing, we will come back to the carpet and share." Show them another picture and label the picture to explain during the Maker's Talk.

Active Involvement: *"Can you close your eyes right now and think of a material or area that will give you inspiration today?"* Pause and give think time. *"Would you open your eyes and tell someone the material or area you would like to play with today? What might you make there today?"* Allow students to turn and talk to each other or to tell adults in the room that they are ready. Allow children to choose which area they would like to go to, and capture their ideas on anecdotal records so you can check in with them during StoryMaking time. If you are implementing StoryMaking at the beginning of the year, then you can limit the choices based on the areas you have opened up to them.

• Voices from the Field •

"One of the things I thought about at the start of this year was WHY did they seem to be further along than the students at this time of the year in previous years. One thing I have done differently is instead of asking the kids during the first few lessons "Where do you want to make your story?" (for example, in housekeeping, in blocks, in science), I basically have modeled a story in one place. For example, during the first few StoryMaking lessons, we all did blocks. As the year progresses, I am going to be letting them chose wherever and whatever they want to make a story, but for the first weeks I am going to be modeling and teaching them how to use a material."

—Lori, integrated pre-K teacher

IMAGINE

Help children think about what materials they want to play with today to help inspire their making. Document their choices on the Status of Stories Documentation Record form (see appendix).

PLAY & MAKE

Visit a few Makerspaces to observe or record or have one-on-one conferences with the children. Prompt to help students discover their stories. Take dictation and a picture of their stories for documentation, or take pictures of students playing with different materials to add to the anchor chart.

SHARE

Bring students back to the meeting area. Move the arrow to the "Share" portion of the anchor chart. *"Now StoryMakers, every day we will end our StoryMaking with a share time. Sometimes we will have one of you come up and share in a Maker's Talk, and sometimes I will share something that I hope you will try. For example, I saw* (insert child's name) *make their story by. . . . Maybe that is something you might try tomorrow. So remember, every time we meet for StoryMaking, we will first gather at the carpet for our lesson. Then we will go off and imagine, play, and make our stories. Finally we will end our time with our share."* Move the arrow around to the different parts of the chart as you summarize the StoryMaking lesson.

After you have taught this initial lesson and the children are coming to the meeting area, choosing a material or area to play and make, and coming back to share stories, it is time to model how to become inspired by materials in your learning environment so students can see a new purpose in their play. Also, once students are used to the routine, retire the "StoryMakers Work Like This . . ." anchor chart and begin to use the StoryMaker Cycle anchor chart, as shown in the next lesson.

Building StoryMaking Strategies

This next lesson is generative, meaning that it can be used again and again with different examples to help children build a comprehensive set of strategies over time on how to play and make with a variety of materials. We recommend starting with a material that your students are most familiar with or interested in. Each learning environment we visited started in a different way. In one classroom, the students couldn't get enough of playing with blocks, so we started modeling with blocks to keep their excitement going. In another classroom, they were ready for a new material to re-engage their excitement for play, so we chose collage. Another Reggio-inspired classroom focused on art materials, because they were learning techniques with their colored pencils. Finally we started some students using toothpicks, low-temperature glue guns, and Styrofoam blocks in a tinkering space, because it was later in the year when they started and these children were used to making in their tinkering space. The point is that no matter what material you choose, you can use the "How to Be a StoryMaker" lesson to support students' new purpose in their play.

---------- STORYMAKING FOCUS LESSON ----------
How to Be a StoryMaker

This is a generative lesson for modeling how to play and make a story with each Makerspace over time (building materials, sewing, collage, weaving, housekeeping, puppets, math manipulatives, science area, art area, water/sand table, playdough).

Objective: Children will share a story from their lives by using materials to make this moment.

MATERIALS

- Blocks with pictures connected to a topic you are investigating
- Books related to a topic you are investigating
- People and other figurines related to your topic; different-sized blocks
- Small anchor chart to place in the center: "What do these blocks/building materials inspire you to make?"
- "How to Be a StoryMaker" anchor chart

- Photos of children playing from a retired "StoryMakers Work Like This . . ." anchor chart
- Your own personal memory connected to materials you chose for your lesson
- Camera to capture documentation
- Status of Stories Documentation Record

FOCUS & EXPLORE

Connect: *"Every day we go to our areas and use our imagination to play. We dress up in housekeeping and imagine we are cooking. We paint and draw pictures and remember special times with our families. We even use blocks and imagine castles and cities to build. We have so much fun! But did you know that playing with these materials could inspire a story to make? I was thinking that today when you go to your areas, you could use the materials and become inspired to make a story. You will learn how to be a STORYMAKER!"*

Teach: *"For example, I will be playing in the block area today. Look at some of these materials."* Show blocks with photos connected to a topic you are studying, people figurines, and other blocks. *"I wonder, 'What do these materials inspire me to make?'"* Model the memory-sharing strategy by retelling your own story. The following example involves looking at a block with a picture of a lake taped to it, but you can substitute your own story using another photo. *"This material makes me remember a time I played in a puddle. This is a story! I can use this block as my setting and make what happened around it. I remember that day I saw a puddle. It was after it rained outside my house. Let me add those details with this material* (start building a house with blocks) *to the structure I'm building. Then I remember jumping in the puddle. Will you help me add to my story?"* Ask a student to help you add the detail to your story using that material. (Allow everyone to participate in building a story to add differentiation.) Add jumping, or another character action, for the rest of the students to act out to keep them engaged.

Active Involvement: Now ask children to share a few examples by pointing to a material and saying the story idea or memory that they connect it to. *"What do these materials inspire you to make?"* Have the children think, then share aloud a few ideas or allow the class to turn and talk.

    "So today you will learn how to be a StoryMaker by imagining a story and playing with materials to help make the story" (point to each part of the chart).

IMAGINE

Ask children, *"Think about what materials you want to play with today to inspire you. When you think you know where you are going to go today, put your thumbs up."* Document using the Status of Stories Documentation Record (see appendix).

PLAY & MAKE

Facilitate a small group at one of the Makerspaces. Prompt to help children discover their stories. Take dictation and photos of their story when they are ready to tell their story. Use one documentation form per child.

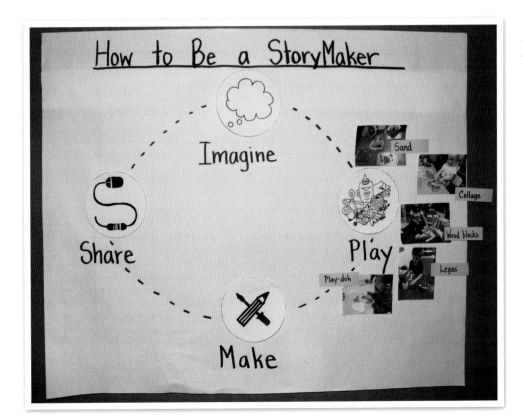

SHARE

Find a few students who made a story to participate in a Maker's Talk and share their story. It is helpful for students to have either a picture or their actual materials with them so they can physically touch the material to help them remember each part. Add documentation of the stories the children make throughout the year.

INTRODUCING A NEW MATERIAL

During Phase 1, it is important not only to model the new purpose of materials students are used to playing with but also to introduce a new material. Introducing a new material will add curiosity and excitement to the children's play. Of course, with any new material, children need ample time to explore it using all of their senses. You will witness children stacking, dumping, and filling with it instead of becoming inspired. Refer to the list on page 84 for child behaviors we observed during Phase 1 of the first unit. These behaviors align with a child's developmental stages of play. Children must be allowed to explore the materials before we can expect them to engage in pretend play or use them imaginatively. For our first new material, we chose to introduce more of a Makerspace material with the use of collage. The question you will want to reinforce with your children is "What do these materials inspire you to make?" To inspire making, we recommend posting a small anchor chart in each of the areas with this question and photos specific to the material in the space. Here is an example of the sign in our collage area.

Collage Makerspace and anchor chart to inspire making

We recommend that you balance your teaching by offering some demonstration-style lessons and some inquiry-style lessons. Kristine Mraz and Christine Hertz summarize the research from Sarah Lewis's *The Rise* (2014) on an experiment around the presentation of a toy. The researchers presented the same toy differently to two groups of children. One group learned how the toy worked through a direct-instruction approach. The other group was given time for open exploration of the toy. "Researchers found that the children who were allowed to explore the toy through play had greater curiosity, engagement, and stamina. They discovered hidden features on the toy that the direct-instruction group overlooked, they played longer, and they worked more collaboratively" (2015, 158). We therefore felt it was important to offer an inquiry-style lesson to support the balance between these two types of needed instruction. Here is an inquiry-style lesson to introduce the new material of collage.

• Voices from the Field •

"I selected these materials because of the interest level of my students. Earlier this week, I told my students I was going to create a new space for them and shared different materials we could put in the space. Their overwhelming decision was to use different collage materials. The collage materials I put out today are different than those we used in Unit 2 and incorporated colors, sizes, and textures they have not used before."

—Tara, integrated pre-K teacher

---------- STORYMAKING FOCUS LESSON ----------
Introducing Collage

Objective: Children will make a story by using collage materials in a new Makerspace.

MATERIALS

- Collage material options (felt pieces, acorns, moss, leaves, wood pieces, gems, bark, feathers, wooden beads, sticks, buttons, and other loose parts)
- Small anchor chart to place in the new Makerspace: "What do these collage materials inspire you to make?"
- Status of Stories Documentation form
- Camera to capture documentation

FOCUS & EXPLORE

Connect: *"Good morning, StoryMakers! StoryMakers sometimes use a technique called collage. Can everyone say collage? I think we all can learn how to become StoryMakers using collage so we can learn a new way to make our stories."*

Teach: *"I'm wondering . . . My question today, StoryMakers, is 'What do these collage materials inspire you to make?'* Show the small anchor chart. *Umm, I don't know. I think we are going to have to inquire and study this together. I brought some special materials with me today for collage. I want you to be thinking about what story this material unlocks* (unlock signal on head) *or makes you think of."*

Show pieces of different-colored felt and look like you are thinking. *"Is anyone inspired? What does this make you think of? Can we make a story like this?"* Allow a few students to share aloud their ideas.

"Wait a minute, do we need more materials to make our story in collage?" Pull out a box or tray of loose parts. Look at these materials. *"I wonder what these materials make you think of?"*

Active Involvement: Continue to pull out a variety of loose parts for students to see. *"StoryMakers, I want you to think. Look at these different materials. What do these collage materials inspire you to make?"* Give think time and then have students turn and talk or share aloud a few responses.

Brooklyn makes her character with collage materials.

IMAGINE

Invite children to think about what materials they want to play with today. Call on students and record which material will help them become inspired and check whether they have a story inspiration on the Status of Stories Documentation Record.

PLAY & MAKE

Observe a small group at the collage Makerspace. Take dictation and a picture of their collage when they have made it and are ready to share their story.

Documentation added to the anchor chart demonstrates the Make component of the StoryMaker Cycle.

SHARE

Find a few students who made a story to share their stories in a Maker's Talk. It is helpful for students to have either a picture or their actual materials with them so they can physically touch the material to help them remember each part. Add collage documentation under the "Make" category of the anchor chart from lesson one.

Teaching StoryMaking Strategies

Of course, it does take a large amount of time for children to question and fully explore the materials before they become inspired. Some children may naturally begin to share stories during play, but we have observed that it is more difficult with some materials. It also may be difficult for some students who haven't experienced play experiences. We have therefore developed an inquiry-style lesson for children to gain strategies on story inspiration ideas.

---------- STORYMAKING FOCUS LESSON ----------

Where Do Story Ideas Come From?
(Multiple-day lesson, 1 to 3 days)

Objective: Children will learn how to come up with a story idea by discovering the ideas of real authors.

MATERIALS

- Book covers of your favorite books
- Chart paper for anchor chart "Where Do Story Ideas Come From?"
- Marker
- Status of Stories Documentation Record
- StoryMaking Documentation Record or StoryMaking Photo Documentation Record
- Camera to capture documentation

FOCUS & EXPLORE

Connect: Day 1: *"We have been working on playing and making our stories using the different materials in our Makerspaces. But sometimes, StoryMakers, we go off and play and play and are stuck on what could be a story. So today we are going to learn where story ideas come from by imagining how authors get their ideas to write books."*

Teach: *"I am wondering, where do story ideas come from? Let's take a look at this book cover."* Show the cover of a book you and your children know very well. For example, you can dis-
play the cover of classics such as *Planting a Rainbow* by Lois Ehlert or *Dear Zoo* by Rod Campbell. *"Wow! StoryMakers, what do you think inspired this author to write about _____?"* Take note of their ideas, and lift the idea that the author may have used their imagination to make a book about their favorite places. Write "favorite places" on the anchor chart, ask students for a few of their favorite places, and sketch examples of them next to this line on the chart.

Anchor chart to inspire story ideas

Option: Depending on the attention span of your children, continue to show a few more book covers, such as *How to Babysit a Grandma* by Jean Reagan and *Biscuit* by Alyssa Satin Capucilli, to suggest that we can make stories about our favorite people and pets. Lift the idea of "favorite people" and write that on the chart. Ask students for a few ideas to sketch or provide picture ideas next to that line. This could also be done on day 2.

Day 2, 3, or later in year: Show another book cover. Lift the idea of "a special time" and "a special object" to add to the anchor chart, with sketches or pictures next to it.

Active Involvement: *"Wow, StoryMakers, our favorite books and authors really helped us out today by showing us where we can imagine stories in our own lives. Now when you're lost for a story idea, we have some strategies to play and make with your materials. Let me know if you discover any other story ideas while you're playing today, and we will add them to the chart."*

IMAGINE

Ask students to turn and talk and make a plan of what story they could tell today and what materials they may be working on. Review your anecdotal notes and check on students to see where they are going and what story they will be working on. Record each student's plan on the Status of Stories Documentation Record.

PLAY & MAKE

Observe students and document any story ideas using either the StoryMaking Documentation Record or the StoryMaking Photo Documentation Record.

SHARE

Find a few students who made a story they would like to share during the Maker's Talk. Ask them to discuss their inspiration and connect to any other authors they know. If any other general story ideas are made (such as a time you had a strong feeling or found a special object), add them to the anchor chart.

- -

Books to Inspire Story Ideas

This lesson can be used throughout the year and anytime you see that your children need inspiration to re-energize their StoryMaking ideas. Mentor texts can help you inspire your children's StoryMaking ideas. Below is just a sample of other books and the inspired story ideas you can lift from them to write on your anchor chart:

Favorite Places
- *The Listening Walk* by Paul Showers
- *Pete the Cat: Pete at the Beach* by James Dean
- *Over in the Meadow* by Olive A. Wadsworth and Ezra Jack Keats

Favorite People
- *The Sandwich Swap* by Queen Rania of Jordan Al Abdullah
- *Clifford the Big Red Dog* by Norman Bridwell

Favorite Food or Restaurant
- *Dragons Love Tacos* by Adam Rubin
- *If You Give a Mouse a Cookie* by Laura Numeroff

A Special Time
- *David Goes to School* by David Shannon
- *We're Going on a Bear Hunt* by Michael Rosen

A Special Object
- *Knuffle Bunny* by Mo Willems
- *Fossil* by Bill Thomson
- *Those Shoes* by Maribeth Boelts

A Strong Feeling
- *The Pout-Pout Fish* by Deborah Diesen
- *Llama Llama Mad at Mama* by Anna Dewdney

TIPS FOR STUDENTS WITH SPECIAL RIGHTS

To make this lesson accessible to all early learners, here are some tips:

- When modeling actions during your StoryMaking, provide the same material for the child to act out. For example, if you modeled your character jumping in a puddle with a figurine, give the child the same type of material and ask them to show you jumping.

- Add sign language for actions into your focus lessons. Sign the action during the modeled play. Provide an image of how to make this sign in your teaching area and ask the child to repeat the sign.

- Create a series of pictures for children to look at before they go to Play & Make. For example, you might have images of a beach, pond, or park. Ask "What type of material are you inspired to make with today?" Allow the child time to point and support her finding and matching materials to play with for that story inspiration.

- Narrate the child's play so he hears a story being told. Give the child an opportunity to share during a Maker's Talk by storytelling what they did. Pause and allow the child to act out the action they just heard you share.

WHAT TO EXPECT DURING PHASE 1 OF YOUR FIRST UNIT

During Phase 1, "Explore," of our StoryMaking units, students are introduced to new materials to inspire stories to play and make. It is also our goal during this time to provide experiences where students develop new inspiration strategies as well as vocabulary. We learned many lessons from the field on what student behaviors could be expected during initial implementation. What follows is a review of the educator roles and expected behaviors from our children during Phase 1.

The goals of StoryMaking Focus Lessons may include the following:

- Introduction of the parts of StoryMaking

- Introduction to a variety of materials for the purpose of imagining a story (blocks, sculpting, housekeeping/dramatic play, art, collage, weaving)

- Ways to come up with story ideas (use of magazines, pictures, decorating folders, mentor texts)

Below are your roles during Phase 1:

- Set up materials and new purpose for play

- Share a story from your own life using a variety of materials

- Build a culture of storytelling throughout the day

- Question students on their story ideas and materials used to help them imagine their stories and get them used to the purpose of StoryMaking Play & Make

- Narrate students' play to model how to share a story idea during their Play & Make

- Recognize that when students are sharing a story with a material, it is time to move on to Phase 2

Here are the child behaviors you may observe during Play & Make:

- Free exploration and curiosity of the materials (such as dump, stack, fill)

- More interest in play than imagining a story

- Jumping from one story idea to another

- Jumping from one area or material to another

- Quickly abandoning a story topic to play with another material

FINAL THOUGHTS

It is hard to know where to start when faced with any new task. We hope that by reading this chapter, you not only understand why it is important to teach making through play but also that you have a tool kit of suggested lessons that will help you on your way. These lessons are scripted to provide support but in no way do we want to send the impression that this is the only "right" way. In the spirit of the maker movement, we encourage you to innovate and make your own versions of the lessons we have provided. We can't wait for educators like you to play, make, and share your way to even better StoryMaking experiences with your children!

Maker's Moment

While Ms. Rachel, a pre-K teacher in a nonverbal and autistic classroom, was checking in with two of her students during StoryMaking, she reminded them about the book they had read earlier. She said, "We read a book about it raining on this little girl and that inspired us to make a story." She then asked Edmundo to show Madison how he imagined it raining with his collage materials which Ms. Rachel had witnessed him playing with earlier. Edmundo dropped the shiny jewels on his felt square.

Ms. Rachel exclaimed, "Whoa, that looked just like rain, didn't it? Can you use any of these characters to make your story?" Edmundo selected a little boy from the figurines and began to make him walk across the blue felt square. He started to narrate his actions, picked up the blue jewels, and dropped them on his head to represent raining. Ms. Rachel proudly said, "Edmundo, you just made a story!" Ms. Rachel asked him to make it again, and this was Edmundo's story:

Edmundo rehearses his story using materials he selected to represent rain.

"He was walking. (Acted out by pouring gems on the head of a boy figure to represent that it rained on him.) *And it rained on his head. And he is getting W E T!"*

CHAPTER 5

Investigating Ways to Grow in StoryMaking

A LESSON IN REMAKING STORIES

For several weeks, the children in Ms. Angela's room had been exploring their materials for the new purpose of imagining story ideas. It was late September, and Ms. Angela and I felt it was time to move on to Phase 2 because we observed children were choosing materials to make their stories. They now began to understand the new purpose for our play and that the materials helped them imagine stories. Therefore, for our focus lesson, we taught the students how to return to their story inspiration, repurpose the materials, and hack into the parts of the story to make it the best version they felt they could share. You will find a sample of this lesson later in the chapter. Before the children chose their new Makerspace, we handed each of them a picture of the story they had made with blocks, playdough, crayons, or other materials. After about forty-five minutes of playing and remaking, a few students wanted to share. Here is what the "Share" sounded like that day.

MS. ANGELA: Today we taught you all about retelling. Retelling is when you tell the same story again, but sometimes you use a different material. I was working with Audrey. I was watching her as a StoryMaker. And she made a story in art today. (*Ms. Angela holds up the piece of work made with crayons and markers to show the class.*) We are going to listen to Audrey tell her story in art. Then she went to blocks. She found the pattern blocks, and she told her story again. She remade her story. So we are going to listen to her two times. She is going to share her story with art, and then she is going to show us how she remade her story with blocks.

AUDREY: A long time ago, me and my dog went in the water and they went in the house and they came back inside. They went in the water again and they sleep and sleep. The end.

MS. ANGELA: Did you hear her story starter?

CLASS: Yeah!

MS. ANGELA: She used "A long time ago." We may have to add that to our chart! So that was her story in art. We are going to hear what she did with the blocks now.

AUDREY: A long time ago, me and my dog saw a big building and we go in the pool. We saw a rainbow and it was pretty. And then we went into the house and back to the water again. Then we went to sleep and sleep and sleep. The end.

MS. ANGELA: Wow! So you can see that when she added the blocks, she was able to tell us a little bit more about her story. She told us about a building and a pool! She added a detail, but it was the same story because her dog went in the water. And then what happened in your story?

AUDREY: They went in the house and went to sleep.

MS. ANGELA: That's right! Would you like a round of applause or a roller-coaster cheer?

AUDREY: Roller-coaster!

The children immediately began clicking their hands going up, up, up to represent the roller coaster and then made three waves down with their hand shouting "Whoo, whoo, whoo" to celebrate Audrey remaking her story with the new materials she chose to play with.

Ms. Angela facilitates Audrey sharing both her original and repurposed story with different materials.

This is such a huge milestone for our early learners when StoryMaking. It is very difficult at first for children at this age to remember the story they made and have the attention span to remake a story either in the same playtime or the following day. Our expectations of the children returning to the "Make" part of our Story-Maker Cycle will increase across the year. Our first goal will be for them to make a story during play and then with our coaching choose another material that same day to hack and repurpose their story. The next goal will be for students to carry over their story idea to the following day. Finally, after we have been engaged in StoryMaking for some time and children have built up their stamina for playing and imagining a story independently in their Makerspaces for at least thirty-five to forty-five minutes or across the days, we will coach them into choosing one of their many stories to revise with new materials. This is modeling the writing process at this early age, and it is successful only if we provide the necessary documentation—by taking photos, recording videos, and transcribing stories—to help children remember their stories. You will find more information on assessment tools and how to document in chapter 7. Children will review their documentation in their StoryMaker folders and express their intention by setting a goal of what story they want to remake and what materials and tools will help them accomplish their goal.

DEVELOPING SKILLS THROUGH TINKERING AND MENTOR TEXTS

During Phase 2, "Investigate," we begin to balance instruction between developing the skills of the maker and of the storyteller or writer. Materials that children explore and tinker with in Phase 1 will now be investigated as children begin to hack and repurpose those same materials in Phase 2. The StoryMaking materials and tools become the foundation for making meaning out of children's ideas. Researchers Karen Wilkinson, Luigi Anzivino, and Mike Petrich (2016) at the Tinkering Studio in San Francisco have noticed that storytelling can be a driving force in the tinkering process. Stories emerge when children work closely with materials. Since people like to tell stories about things that are important in their lives, materials provide a powerful language for expression. Refer to chapter 2 for help in choosing a new material or tool that can unlock the creativity and imagination for your children to continue to work on their stories. It will re-engage and re-energize their StoryMaking process.

Another powerful way to move our StoryMaking process forward is through the use of mentor texts during focus lessons. "Mentor texts are pieces of literature that we can return to again and again as we help our young writers learn how to do what they may not yet be able to do on their own" (Dorfman and Cappelli 2007, 2–3). When using mentor texts, the child has to first know the story as a reader. That way there is lesson focus on the plot and what is going to happen next, allowing the child to focus on the craft we want to imitate or borrow. Mentor texts help StoryMakers reinvent themselves as storytellers and, eventually, as writers. In this chapter you will see an example of how we use mentor texts to help children share their stories by giving them language on how to start their story. But mentor texts are rich with crafts that show children how to make their stories even better. Ways we have used mentor texts include beginning and ending a story, adding details by describing or drawing the characters' actions and dialogue, and making characters and settings.

Studying the words is not the only way we can use mentor texts. The illustrations are equally as important in developing our StoryMakers. Katie Wood Ray (2010) explains that children make pictures not because they don't know how to write yet; they make pictures because they understand that drawing pictures makes meaning with the words, like the authors and illustrators of the picture books in their room. Mentor texts can be part of the children's reading corner, to be browsed through and read during StoryMaking, after they have been used in focus lessons.

Developing the Maker, the Storyteller, the Artist, and the Writer

During Phase 2 our goal is to coach and guide children into using their everyday materials for new purposes, or to "hack and repurpose," as Peter Wardrip and Lisa Brahms (2015) call it. We want them to return to a story they have made and imagine how to make it better, just like writers revise their work. At this point in the units, however, we have discovered that different groups of children need different things to grow. Since the benefits of StoryMaking are to develop the maker, the storyteller, the artist, and even the writer, teachers need to choose the focus lessons that best meet the needs of their children. For example, one group of children may be proficient at making stories with loose parts, but their illustrations are difficult to interpret. The teacher may decide to plan a focus lesson on drawing shapes to represent characters or to introduce smaller brushes to model how to make details to develop the artist side of the StoryMaker. Another group of children may need to investigate how to begin their stories using mentor texts to develop their writer skills. We will provide focus lessons (both demonstration and inquiry) to help Story-Makers improve their stories by using strategies from the maker and the writing worlds of research.

Below are lesson objectives that help children develop their maker, artist, and writer skills:

- **Maker skills.** Hacking and repurposing materials to better represent an element in their story. For example, a child uses a button to make a sun in her story but then wants to use string and feathers to make the sun rise to show that it is a very sunny day.

- **Maker/writer skills.** Expressing intention by articulating a plan for how they want to use their materials for the purpose of adding to, revising, or deleting parts of their story. For example, "I'm going to use the glue gun and Styrofoam to build my house." "I'm going to use the collage materials to remake my bunny story."

- **Maker/artist skills.** Seeking out resources (books or images) to make their story into an illustration, such as adding setting details to pictures or facial expressions to characters to match their feelings.

- **Writer skills.** Seeking out resources (books) to imagine new ways to begin a story, such as starting with the weather, time of day, or the first thing that a character says or does.

KEEPING LEARNERS ENGAGED WITH NEW MATERIALS OR MAKERSPACES

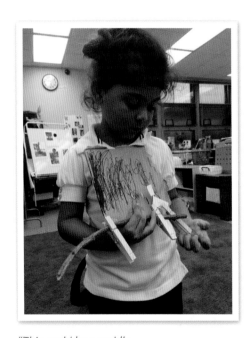

"This could be a paddle. This could be a sail," said Amariah as she picked up and touched each material trying to repurpose how she could use them for her story.

As you go through the StoryMaking process with children, they may show a lack of interest in the same areas or materials. Just as toddlers become bored with their toys at home and the parents have to implement some kind of toy rotation, teachers need to re-engage their little ones by introducing new materials. You may also keep most of the same materials but choose to reorganize them or present them in a new way. For example, during our first unit, which lasted about nine weeks, we had a collage Makerspace with mostly loose parts materials from nature (acorns, moss, wood pieces, gems, shells). For the full nine weeks, we were going to focus on colors and feelings in our stories. We added new materials, such as pom-poms, glass beads, pipe cleaners, and feathers, but organized them in separate boxes according to color to add new interest to the area.

If you choose to introduce art mediums across the year, then Ann Pelo's *The Language of Art* (2017) suggests a range of materials that increase in difficulty of use and technique. Pelo reminds us that children need to be invited to fully explore a new art medium with all their senses before they can use that art medium for representation. For example, when we introduce new materials to an existing Makerspace in the first lesson below, children describe what they imagine using their materials for before they can fully remake their story. We've also found that when children don't know where to go next with their story or materials, they will go back to something they are comfortable with—drawing.

Remaking a Story Using New Materials

Below you will find an example of how we introduced new materials to the existing Makerspace for the purpose of remaking a story. The goal of this lesson is to provide children with an opportunity to reimagine their story by using new materials to hack, repurpose, and revise. You may present the materials in either a demonstration-style lesson by modeling how you made a story or in an inquiry-style lesson by asking children what they can make with the materials. There is no wrong or right way. From our experience when you model how to make an object for your story, such as a boat, be prepared for a lot of boat stories that week! There is nothing wrong with this method, because children will imitate before they learn how to make through their own experiences. But if you are introducing a new tool (low-temperature glue gun, tie wraps, screwdriver) to a Makerspace, then you will want to model the use of the tool so the children can use it properly and safely and can concentrate on the materials to help them imagine their new version of their story.

> **• Voices from the Field •**
>
> "One of the most exciting things is that this gives our students an opportunity to explore materials and create freely. They can use their imaginations, make their stories using a variety of materials, and they are not bound by normal conventions. StoryMaking gives them opportunities to expand their oral-language vocabulary, improve their storytelling skills, and take risks they might not normally take."
>
> —Tara, integrated pre-K teacher

Inquiry-style anchor charts ask guiding questions such as, "What stories can we imagine with these new materials?" and "How can these new materials help us remake our stories?"

---------- STORYMAKING FOCUS LESSON ----------
New Materials in Our
Attachments Makerspace

Objective: Children will return to a story idea by choosing new materials to remake their story.

MATERIALS

- Tie wraps, string, twigs, binder clips, rubber bands, pipe cleaners
- Construction paper
- Scissors
- Tape
- StoryMaking documentation form of your choice
- Camera to capture documentation

FOCUS & EXPLORE

Connect: *"We have been learning how materials can help us imagine and make stories. Is there a material that really helps you imagine a story in your mind?"* Ask children to turn and talk to each other to reflect on their explorations, or invite a few children to share. For example, one child told our group that he thought housekeeping had helped him make a story. I asked what kind of materials in that space had helped him, and he told us the food. I prompted him and asked what the food had made him think of and he said a shopping cart of full of food. I reminded him that he could make a story about that. *"You have been working with tools that help you attach and make things, such as tape and rubber bands. Today I would like to show you a new tool called a tie wrap."*

Teach: Introduce the tie wrap and demonstrate how to use the tool to connect objects. Then pull out some new materials and display them in front of the children. (Attachments Makerspace examples are cardboard, string, sticks, clothespins, pipe cleaners, twine; housekeeping examples are paint chips, rulers, bandanas, water sensory bottles.)

"Today I want to show you some new materials, and I want you to be thinking, 'How can these materials help me remake my story?' Can we all be investigators today by helping me think of how I can play and make with these materials?"

First present the materials one at a time and have students repeat what they are called. Next present each new material and ask students to investigate it. Create an inquiry-style anchor chart and write down what the children can imagine and make with each material.

Active Involvement: Ask children to look at all the things they said they could make from the list on the chart. Give each child a photograph of the last story they made. Ask *"How can these materials help you remake your story?"* Prompt students to find a detail from their story and then explain how they can remake that object, action, or person.

IMAGINE

Ask children to turn and talk and make a plan of what they might remake today and what materials will help them. Review your anecdotal notes, and check on children to see what story they will be continuing.

PLAY & MAKE

Document the stories children remake by taking pictures and dictation.

SHARE

Find a student who used a new material to share with the group.

- -

HOW TO STAY ORGANIZED

When we first developed the StoryMaking process and had guided children into remaking their stories, we quickly faced a new problem: What do we do with all this photo and recorded story documentation? We needed a way for our children to have access to their work so they could refer to it to make meaningful decisions as they played. We took inspiration from the writing world and introduced a StoryMaking folder for each child. We discovered that throughout any unit you teach, you might have to insert a management focus lesson to move the StoryMaking process along.

Two-pocket, three-prong folders make good StoryMaking folders. Below are some ideas on creating StoryMaking folders and organizing documentation in them:

Cover: Create a cover of your choice. You may even give the students the opportunity to decorate their covers with possible story ideas (clip art, photos that remind them of stories).

Inside-left pocket: Place a green dot or picture icon on the pocket. Pictures of student's stories made with materials, illustrations, and writing paper of stories they want to continue to work on will go in this pocket.

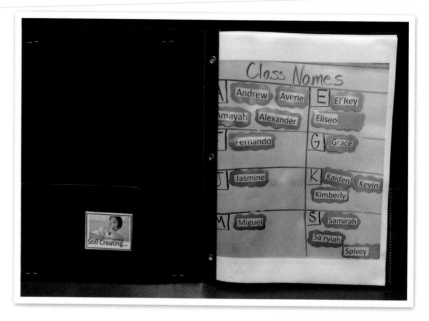

Inside-center section: Place copies of an alphabet chart or a name chart in the center section to help students with writing. This should be the same chart you use for phonics instruction. Place copies of all anchor charts created for this unit, such as parts of a StoryMaking time chart, and charts on story ideas, how to start a story, how to make a story, and how to publish a story in this section too.

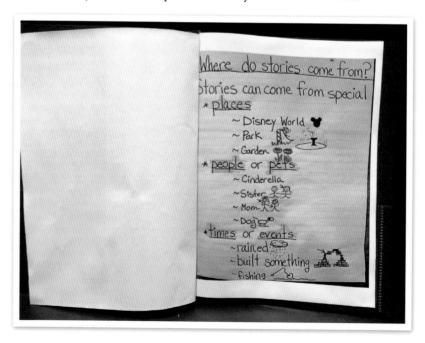

Inside-right pocket: Place a red dot or picture icon on the pocket. Pictures of students' stories made with materials, illustrations, and writing paper of stories they are finished working on will go in this pocket.

Children use the charts in their StoryMaking folders to write their stories.

• **Voices from the Field** •

What excites you about StoryMaking?

"It's open ended, there is no right or wrong, and they can build on their stories from week to week. It will help the students organize their thoughts and make it an easier transition when writing their stories on paper. Learning to communicate their ideas will help them gain self-confidence in future learning environments."

—Lori, integrated pre-K teacher

---------- STORYMAKING FOCUS LESSON ----------
Introducing StoryMaker Folders

Objective: Children will organize their documentation by using their own StoryMaker folder.

MATERIALS

- Documentation of students' ongoing work (pictures or actual pieces from Makerspaces)
- Two-pocket, three-prong folders, one for each student
- One StoryMaker folder you have created with documentation of your own story
- Status of Stories Documentation Record

FOCUS & EXPLORE

Connect: Reflect on the learning your children have been working on or any noticings you would like to share. *"StoryMakers, we have been working on so many stories, and I have been taking your pictures and recording your stories, but we have a problem! What are we going to do with all this paper? Some of you have even written or painted your stories, but you have nowhere to put them. So I want to show you how to keep track of your stories by using your very own StoryMaker folder!"*

Teach: Present the folder and tell why it is important. *"This is a very special tool and I want you to watch how I can use this to organize all of my papers."* Open up the folder and show children the inside pockets. The inside pocket should have a "still creating" clip art note or a green dot attached to it. Explain that this means "go." The back pocket should have an "all done" clip art note, a red stop sign, or a red dot that means "stop." *"Watch me to see how I am going to organize my stories."* Take out examples of documentation and remind them of the story. *"This is my story of a time I [add topic of your story]. I have been working on this story for a while now. I don't think I want to make it anymore, so where do you think I should place it in my folder? In the pocket with the green 'go' sign that says I want to keep working on it or in the back pocket with the red 'stop' sign that means I want to stop?"* Continue this process with a few different pieces of your own documentation until you feel children understand the purpose. Don't worry about explaining the center section of charts. You will use them with students when you speak with them during their Play & Make.

Active Involvement: Give students their own folder and a piece of documentation to organize. Observe students organizing their paper and ask how they are going to use their StoryMaking folders.

IMAGINE

Use your Status of the Stories Documentation Record to note the children's plan for the day. Prompt children to show you what story they will be continuing to make by pointing to the documentation in their StoryMaking folder.

PLAY & MAKE

Document the stories children remake by taking pictures and dictation. You may give children their documentation to organize with support. Throughout the weeks, use this time to place mini-versions of the anchor charts in the room so they always have access to their previous learning.

SHARE

Select a few students who made a story to show how they will organize their documentation.

HELPING CHILDREN MAKE A PLAN FOR STORYMAKING

Another thing we can learn from the maker research is that children begin to express intention with how they will use their materials for a personalized project or for a new imagined creation (Wardrip and Brahms 2015). Gever Tulley (2009) explains that sometimes children start from doodles and sketches, make real plans, or just start building. Building is at the heart of their experience just as making is the heart of our StoryMaking experience. Here is a lesson that will guide children in making a plan before they play and make in order to express intention for their work that day. It is connected to our color and feelings unit, but you can change the categories to match the needs of your own children.

---------- **STORYMAKING FOCUS LESSON** ----------
Imagine Before You Play

Objective: Children will imagine stories before they play by using an anchor chart to express intention.

MATERIALS

- Anchor chart: "Imagine Before You Play"
- Clip art with labels for students to choose
- Your plan that includes a person and action with matching materials to demonstrate a story
- StoryMaking documentation form of your choice
- Camera to capture documentation

Changes in the "Imagine Before You Play" anchor chart throughout the year

FOCUS & EXPLORE

Connect: *"We have been using new materials to either remake our stories or imagine new stories to make. However, I noticed that when we start to play, we sometimes forget what we are making. We forget about our stories. Therefore, today we are going to learn how to plan and imagine our stories before we play."*

Teach: Show students the chart and explain that these are only some options in the "Who" and "What" columns and that they can use their imaginations to add even more ideas. For example, you could say, *"Here's a plan that we can use before we play. The first thing we can do is choose a character. Characters are the people or animals in our story. So here are some ideas, and I want you to be thinking, 'Who can I imagine in my story?'"* Go through each picture so students are exposed to the vocabulary and possible choices for their play. *"Who could I make my story about today?"* Take ideas from the children to see if they understand the meaning of characters and select one (such as "me"). Then move on to the next column on the chart. *"Now I have to have some actions in my story."* Present pictures and labels. *"What do you think I [or the character] should do in my story?"* Take ideas from the children and select one (such as "slip and fall"). You can add any other column based on your unit objectives. For example, during our color and feelings unit, we added a feelings category and the children picked "embarrassed." Restate the plan and ask children what material they think will help them make their story. Take ideas and select one (such as blocks).

Active Involvement: Go get the chosen materials to make your story in front of the children. Be sure to think aloud about what you can make with each material you touch. Say *"This could be me,"* as you select a figurine out of the basket. Say *"This could be a water table,"* as you stack blue blocks to make that detail in the story.

Share your story inspired by the materials. For example, *"One morning, I went to class and wanted to play in the water tub. I went with some friends and we played and played. The water splashed out and made a puddle on the floor. It was time to clean up, so I walked around and slipped and fell on the puddle. Then I felt embarrassed."*

IMAGINE

Ask, *"StoryMakers, did you see how this chart helped me get straight to work on making my story? So I want you to think about who your story is going to be about and what they are going to do. Use the chart to help you."* Have students turn and talk to each other to share their plan. Go around and write down their plans on anecdotal records. Then release them to go play and make.

PLAY & MAKE

Document the stories children remake or the new stories they make by taking pictures and taking dictation.

SHARE

Find a student who followed through with his plan to share with the group.

Teacher Tip: Continue to add or replace columns on your charts to help children imagine new possibilities for their stories across the year.

- -

USING BOOKS TO TEACH STORYMAKING

During Phase 2, you will want to provide children with a few strategies to improve their oral storytelling. Studying the words in mentor texts serves as powerful models for students to replicate in their own stories. We noticed that our students didn't know how to start their stories. They sometimes just stared at us, waiting for us to get them going, or they jumped right into explaining what they had made. For example, if Audrey from the beginning of the chapter hadn't used this strategy, she would have told her story like this: "This is the big building and this is the pool and this is my dog. The dog went in the water and in the house to sleep and sleep and sleep" while pointing to everything she had made. We needed to teach the children a strategy to help their oral language develop more into a storyteller's voice. You can go through the books you have in your classroom, check out books at the library, or visit an app with children's stories to find a variety of ways to start a story.

---------- STORYMAKING FOCUS LESSON ----------

How to Start Your Story

Objective: Children will tell a story by using mentor texts to help them know how to start.

MATERIALS

- Documentation of children's ongoing work (pictures or actual pieces from Makerspaces)
- A story of your own that your children know well
- Mentor texts that show a variety of ways to begin a story
- Copies of the first page of each book used
- "How to Start My Story" anchor chart
- StoryMaking documentation form of your choice
- Camera to capture documentation

FOCUS & EXPLORE

Connect: *"We have learned to make a story and remake the same story using different materials. This is so important because you are planning out what details you really want in your story by making them again and again. But sometimes, StoryMakers, after I create my story using the materials, I kind of freeze up when it's time to tell my story out loud. I just don't know how to start."*

"How to Start My Story" anchor chart

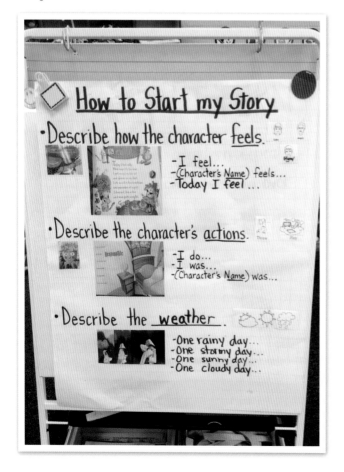

Teach: *"So today I thought we would look to some of our favorite books to help me know how I could start a story. Let's look at this book."* Read the first page of *Rain Fish* by Lois Ehlert, *Snowmen at Night* by Caralyn Buehner, or another mentor text of your choosing that demonstrates how to start a story with the weather. *"Oh, wow, StoryMakers! I could start a story too by describing what the weather was like. Let me try it out with this story."* Show children documentation or a picture of one of the stories they had seen you create from a previous mini-lesson.

Write "Start with the weather" on the anchor chart (add a picture clue).

Option: Depending on the attention span of your children, continue to show another book or wait until day 2. *"Let me see how this author started their book."* Read the first page of *Creak! Said the Bed* by Phyllis Root, *The Grouchy Ladybug* by Eric Carle, or another mentor text of your choosing that shows how to begin a story with the time of day. *"Well, that's a good idea!*

I think I could start my story with the time of day too. Let me try. One dark night. . . ." Continue oral storytelling using documentation of your own story.

Add "Start with the time" to the anchor chart (add a picture clue).

Continue this lesson for another day, or teach new ways to start a story later in the year and add to the anchor chart. See the list of ideas and suggested books at the end of this lesson.

Active Involvement: *"Let's look at what [child's name] created a few days ago. Can you tell us what this story is about?"* Have the child point to the picture or documentation to say who the characters are, where they are, and what they are doing.

"StoryMakers, can you help us out? How do you think we should start the story? Should we start like the author in this book or in this book? Or do you have a completely new idea in your imagination?" Ask children to turn and talk to a partner and explain why they should choose that way to start the story. Then coach the child into telling the story using one of the starters.

"Wow, StoryMakers, our author friends really helped us out today! Now we have some strategies when we don't know how to start. When we are stuck on how to begin sharing our story, we can say (use examples from anchor chart). *Let me know if you find any other ways to begin, and we can add those ideas to our anchor chart."*

IMAGINE

Ask students to turn and talk and make a plan of what story they might tell today and what materials they will be working on. Review your anecdotal notes, and check on children to see where they are going and what story they will be working on.

PLAY & MAKE

Document the stories students share by recording pictures and dictation on a StoryMaking documentation form of your choice.

SHARE

Find a child who used a story starter and allow them to share.

The list below of ways to start a story and suggested mentor texts can be used to plan your lessons. Feel free to add your own titles to make your units specific to your needs and children's interests.

Start with the time of day
- *Moondance* by Frank Asch
- *The Snowy Day* by Ezra Jack Keats
- *Fireflies* by Julie Brinckloe

Start with the weather
- *Blizzard* by John Rocco
- *The Wind Blew* by Pat Hutchins

Start by describing a place
- *It's Mine* by Leo Lionni
- *Bear Snores On* by Karma Wilson
- *Goodnight Moon* by Margaret Wise Brown

Start with a sound
- *Feathers for Lunch* by Lois Ehlert
- *Little Blue Truck* by Alice Schertle

Start with dialogue
- *Ralph Tells a Story* by Abby Hanlon
- *Come On, Rain!* by Karen Hesse

Using Illustration to Add Detail to Stories

Another way to use books is through illustration studies. We adapted this lesson from Katie Wood Ray's *In Pictures and In Words* (2010) to study with students how we can add nature details into our own illustrations and make our settings come alive. Her book is full of wonderful lessons that you can use to study illustrators, or you can be an investigator, study the illustrations from your own favorite books, and annotate the pages for yourself.

---------- STORYMAKING FOCUS LESSON ----------
Illustration Study on Adding Details

Objective: Children will add details to their illustrations by studying the work of other illustrators.

MATERIALS

- Documentation of students' ongoing work (pictures or actual pieces from Makerspaces)
- Mentor text (*Flashlight* by Lizi Boyd, *The Little Gardener* by Emily Hughes, the One Small Square series by Donald M. Silver, or other texts with nature details in the illustrations)
- Sticky notes
- Marker
- StoryMaking documentation form of your choice
- Camera to capture documentation

FOCUS & EXPLORE

Connect: *"We have been learning many strategies from the authors on our bookshelf about how we can make our stories even better. But do you know there is another person involved in making a book? The illustrator is the person who makes the illustrations or pictures in the book. They are equally important to making the story. Today we are going to study the illustrations to see how we can make our pictures clearer for our audience."*

Teach: Show students a page from the book and ask, *"What details from nature do you see in this picture?"* Model pointing out a few examples and writing those details on a sticky note.

Here is an annotated mentor text example from Noah Chases the Wind by Michelle Worthington.

Active Involvement: Invite children to explain what details they see, and write down their answers on sticky notes to annotate the illustration.

IMAGINE

Prompt children to look in their StoryMaking folders to choose whether they are going to remake a story today or imagine a new story to play and make. Ask a few children to share what they are going to do or allow time for them to turn and talk to a friend. Review your anecdotal notes and check on children to see where they are going and what story they will be working on.

PLAY & MAKE

You may want every child to try this new strategy and create an illustration or allow them to choose which material they want to play and make. You will document the stories children make by collecting their illustration and recording dictation.

SHARE

Find a few children who made an illustration to share. Have the children find the nature details in their illustrations and allow time for compliments.

TIPS FOR STUDENTS WITH SPECIAL RIGHTS

We have found that it sometimes takes a long time to record all the children's plans before they go off and play. And some of our students do not access the language to orally communicate their plan. One teacher, Laurie Funderburk, came up with an idea to insert the planning pages in the center of the StoryMaking folders. She placed each page in a page protector, and children used a dry-erase marker to quickly make their own plan. Then, as she and her assistant checked in with children during their playing, she could observe whether they were staying with their plan or talk about why they changed their plan for their new purpose.

Children can circle a plan for making in their StoryMaking folder prior to playing.

In our nonverbal autistic classroom, we needed a better way for students to plan so all students had access to StoryMaking. One teacher, Rachel Spivey, used Board-maker to create storyboards for students to plan their stories. Then students could use the pages to find the materials in the room and play. This allowed all children to have access to the StoryMaking experience and choose characters, actions, and feelings for their stories.

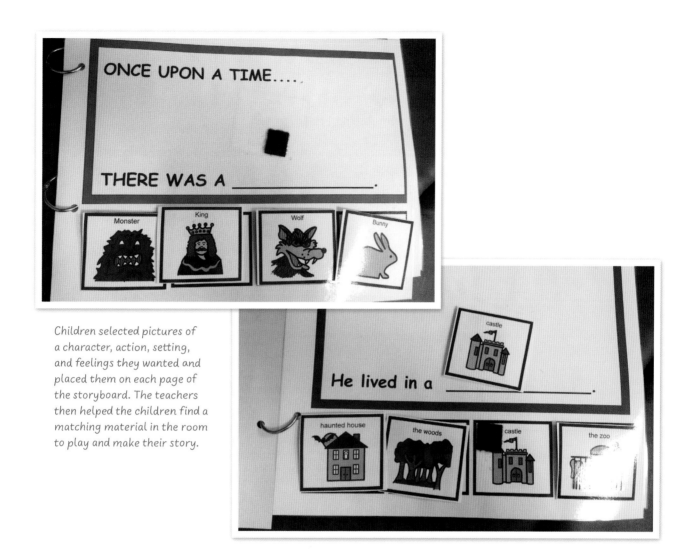

Children selected pictures of a character, action, setting, and feelings they wanted and placed them on each page of the storyboard. The teachers then helped the children find a matching material in the room to play and make their story.

WHAT TO EXPECT DURING PHASE 2 OF YOUR FIRST UNIT

During Phase 2, "Investigate," of our StoryMaking units, children are invited to re-imagine their stories and return to their materials. The purpose of this phase is for children to try different versions of their story (revising) by repurposing materials they have already used to represent an added or changed detail in their story. Below is a list that highlights educator roles and observed behaviors from our children that you may expect during your implementation.

The goals of the StoryMaking Focus Lessons may include the following:

- Remaking a story by repurposing materials or using different materials to make the same story

- Revising a story by adding more details using different materials

- Using mentor texts to investigate "How can we begin our stories?"

- Introducing writing folders by modeling where to organize stories in pockets

Below are your roles during Phase 2:

- Use documentation tools and anecdotal records to record children's stories

- Observe and record students' stories and the frequency of the materials they use

- Record pictures for documentation

Here are the child behaviors you may observe during Play & Make:

- May remake the story, but only very quickly, then shares the brief story and is done in a short time span

- Remakes the story, but when tinkering with a different material, may then share a completely different version of the story

- Is eager to build and get their picture taken with their story because of the newness of documentation

- Views pictures of their story creations to scaffold the revisiting of their story from day to day

- Expresses great excitement and enthusiasm to share their stories and show off their story creation

FINAL THOUGHTS

The heart of this chapter is about showing educators how to plan Phase 2 instruction and lead students into deeper levels of investigation with a specific story. Children will learn to remake a story by trying different versions of the same idea with different materials. They will also become more proficient StoryMakers by developing their own skills as makers, storytellers, artists, or writers. The role of the mentor text is also a powerful tool to move our StoryMakers forward. We want to coach children during this phase to remake and revise stories by repurposing and hacking materials to make the best version of their story. When they are proud of what they have made, we will facilitate different ways they can share their creations and stories with the world!

Maker's Moment

Ms. Lori introduced illustration studies to her students. They used a favorite book to learn how to add nature details to their stories. Here is the dictation she took for Bowden's story:

Bowden illustrates his first version of his story.

"Once upon a time, it was a sunny day and Vito was in his cave. Then it started to get dark. And he looked outside of his cave and he saw dark clouds and it started to rain so he went back inside."

The next day the children remade their stories using different materials. Bowden chose to remake his story using Legos. Here is the dictation his teacher recorded:

"Once upon a time, Vito was inside a cave. Then all of his friends come. And then Vito was outside behind his cave and it was trying to rain. Then fire ants came out. On the bottom of the cave there were rocks. The white guy had this white thing in his hands and was killing the ants and the ants went underground. Then all his friends went into the cave. And then the one ant was still up. Then the white guy got out and sprayed him and it hurt him. The ants went underground. The end."

Bowden remakes his story, adding new details with Legos.

CHAPTER 6

Finding Ways for Children to Communicate Their Learning

A RITUAL FOR COMMUNICATING STORIES

The children in Ms. Katie's class had been making and remaking stories for a few months now. They had established a culture of StoryMaking and were eager to share their stories every day. Maker's Talks were now a common ritual in her classroom, and the children loved to gather back on the carpet after making their stories to explain and tell what happened in their story and to use the materials in front of their peers to show what they had made. Let's take a look into a learning environment to see one way sharing could look for your children.

MS. KATIE: Mason, what area did you start out with today to make a story?

MASON: Water.

MS. KATIE: The water area! And were you playing with the materials in your water area?

MASON: (*nods head and grins*)

MS. KATIE: You were! Wait, should I go get those materials? (*Ms. Katie brings back the materials he was playing with to show the group.*) Mason was playing in the water area and found these three things. What three things did you find?

MASON: Water, a guy, and a hot tub. (*Mason points to the objects in the clear measuring cup to explain to the class.*)

MS. KATIE: A hot tub! He found a hot tub in the water area! So Mason, what was your guy doing in the hot tub?

MASON: The guy put snack in there.

MS. KATIE: And what else? What was he feeling?

MASON: The guy put snacks in there and it got boring.

MS. KATIE: And was he scared or was he relaxed?

MASON: Scared.

MS. KATIE: Why was he scared in the hot tub?

MASON: Because he had boo-boos. (*Mason holds up his illustration that he made about his story and points to that detail in his story.*)

MS. KATIE: So what was happening?

MASON: The boo-boos came off!

MS. KATIE: What are you going to do with your story tomorrow? How is he going to feel?

MASON: Sad.

MS. KATIE: Why will he be sad tomorrow?

MASON: Because I'm going to put crocodiles in there.

MICHELLE: So it looks like you want to keep working on that story. Can you show everyone where you would put that in your StoryMaking folder?

MASON: Right here! (*He places his illustration in the "still working" side of his Story-Making folder. Ms. Katie will add a picture of what he made today to add to his story tomorrow.*)

MICHELLE: That's right! So tomorrow you can remake your story and maybe you can take it to paper since you have made it with two different materials.

Ms. Katie supports Mason sharing his story during a Maker's Talk.

We have many choices when it comes to our children sharing their own stories. Sharing doesn't always have to be in an oral or written form. In this chapter we will describe the different ways that students can share. We will also explore what it means to "Communicate" in Phase 3, where children have a variety of options to share their story with others, and we will broaden our understanding of what it means to publish.

CHILDREN SHARE STORIES THROUGH TALKING, WRITING, AND PUBLISHING

One way that we can share is by telling our stories orally. Oral language is one of many modes of communication through which young children begin to develop proficiency during their early years. The developmental continuum shows that young children can be proficient in their talk and vocabulary usage, employ listening and understanding strategies, participate in acceptable social interactions, be involved in extended discussions, and consider oral-language content in their thinking (ask questions, make predictions, talk about what they know, share knowledge of story structure, describe people and places in a story) (Honig 2007; Pinnell and Fountas 2011). StoryMaking provides a supportive framework to move all types of oral language forward on the continuum of learning in all domains, and it answers to Alice Honig's statement that "encouraging storytelling is particularly urgent" given the diverse needs and cultures represented in our classrooms of early learners (2007, 602). In StoryMaking, storytelling becomes part of the daily routine during which many of the thinking dispositions and making practices are enacted. Storytelling has been considered by some to be a rehearsal for writing, but we believe it is much more than that. We believe that imagining, playing, making, and sharing stories employs thinking dispositions that will be required of children to successfully build the stories of their lives.

Storytelling is a bridge to writing. During Phase 3 of our inquiry framework, we model how to take our stories to paper, where children have the opportunity to select a story to write. Kristin Rainville and Bill Gordh (2016) assert that "children who tell stories are already writers" (79), and when educators share their stories and encourage children to record their own stories, they are creating a community of writers. Children can "publish" the stories that they choose to share by drawing and writing both digitally and on paper. It's important that children be in learning environments where writing is presented as an opportunity to share rather than an assignment.

Teaching children how to take their story to paper through the support of modeled and shared writing opportunities is a developmentally appropriate way for children to learn concepts about print. Marie Clay (2000) explains that when children participate in authentic literacy experiences, they learn concepts about print, such as how printed words tell a story. StoryMaking provides the perfect recipe for children to experiment and explore by making pictures, marks, and letter-like forms to communicate their message. Lucy Calkins (1994) reminds us that adults separate writing from art, song, and play into exercises on lined paper while children see writing as an exploration with marker and pen. By including these developmentally appropriate writing opportunities into the StoryMaking process, children learn that when they make marks on paper—whether scribbles or drawing—their marks hold meaning and convey a message (Rainville and Gordh 2016).

Publishing and sharing a story go beyond just the oral and written opportunities. When students go public, there are so many options for telling it to the world. Print and conversations are just two of the ways, but what about paint, music, drama, sculpture, or even digital storytelling? The ways to communicate are endless. Loris Malaguzzi, founder of Reggio Emilia, summarized it best when he said, "I do not want to limit the domain of symbolic languages only to reading, writing, and numbers. Symbols are used as well by musicians, storytellers and others" (1998, 93).

SHARING STORIES THROUGH MAKER'S TALKS

To develop children's oral language, we end the share portion of our StoryMaking time with a Maker's Talk. This extension of our cycle was inspired by our former work with our teachers to implement project work units across our classrooms. For example, when we were studying a unit on nature, we would hold science talks in order for children to share their experiences and thinking on science concepts. They would have the opportunity to listen to others' theories and make connections to what they already knew and what they were learning. Ingrid Chalufour and Karen Worth (2003) explain in their *Young Scientist Series* that the educator's role is to use children's documentations and representations as a springboard for these conversations. We have found the same process to be effective in StoryMaking. Instead of asking children to share their thinking on science concepts, such as what living things they notice during a nature walk, we encourage them to not only tell their stories but also explain how they were made and what inspired them, and to seek additional resources to make the stories stronger. Below are some tips for a successful Maker's Talk:

- Arrange a special chair or spot in the classroom to create an honored, fun place to share.

Children share their stories with each other using their materials during a Maker's Talk.

- Choose a child who has demonstrated the focus lesson of the day to reinforce and summarize your teaching point (tried a new way to start their story based on the mentor text inspiration, used new materials to make their story).

- Allow the child to bring up her materials to act out and share how she made her story.

- Give children access to the pictures you took of their stories so they can share each part.

- Provide supportive language such as "This is a picture of the story you made. Can you tell us about the story you made?" "Can you point to the parts of your story?" "Can you act out what happened in the story?"

- Start slowly with five-minute talks and gradually increase the time as the children's stamina and attention increase.

- Invite children into the discussion by asking, "What do you think?"

- After routines are in place, establish a sign-up board to encourage children to take ownership of when they want to go public with their story ideas.

RESPONDING TO ONE ANOTHER'S STORIES

It is important to spend time teaching children how to respond to one another's writing and how to support one another in the culture of StoryMaking you have established. To teach the children to give praise to one another may seem like a natural first step, but Lucy Calkins (1994) recommends an alternative to compliments. She describes a scene that she witnessed involving a little girl watching two boys playing around in the water fountain. The little girl ran to her writing folder and pulled out her piece of writing and reminded the boys that her words said, "No fooling around in the water fountain!" The children's teacher had created a culture where the children knew their words meant something. We want children to know that their writing has power. Calkins recommends that instead of giving compliments, we guide children toward asking questions about each other's writing. "When a teacher asks, 'What will you do with your story?' it is a far better compliment than any amount of praise, and it's the kind of compliment that lets children see that writing has its own rewards. . . . When we respect children's early writing, we create a mood of appreciation in the classroom" (70). We recommend doing this whether children are sharing their piece of writing, an oral story, or the actual representation of their story made from materials. Children can be taught how to support each other's StoryMaking by first asking questions during Maker's Talks as well as when they are working at Makerspaces to build their stories.

1. Teach children how to ask questions by pointing to the piece of work and asking, "What is this in your story?" "What is happening?" "What do you want to do with your story?"

2. Later, teach students how to give a compliment by asking, "What was your favorite part?" Give children a language frame for responding ("I like the part . . .").

3. Finally, model how to offer advice ("I think you should . . .") and how the StoryMaker could respond ("I'll think about it," "No thank you," or "That's a good idea, thank you!").

When you check in with children to observe and record their stories, find a small group or pair of children to coach. Suggest to a child that they can help their friend with making their story by asking questions. Here was the very first conversation two children had with this type of support after I prompted one of the children to ask her friend questions about the story she was making.

SARAI: I have a question for you. Who's that? (*Points to a part of her friend's collage.*)

MARIELIS: My mom.

SARAI: What is she doing?

MARIELIS: She's playing in the snow and there's some popcorn.

SARAI: Did you say there was some popcorn?

(*Marielis nods her head in agreement.*)

SARAI: So what's this? (*Points to another detail in the collage.*)

MARIELIS: That's her feet.

SARAI: (*Sarai continues pointing and asking questions about each part and then asks:*) What does she look like?

MARIELIS: A person.

SARAI: I mean, what does her body look like or her dress? What's her favorite color?

MARIELIS: Rainbow color.

SARAI: You mean the whole rainbow? My favorite color is red.

MARIELIS: My favorite color is red too.

Because they get a bit off track, Michelle chimes in to offer a suggestion.

MICHELLE: Could we ask, "How are you going to start your story?" Remember the different ways that we learned?

SARAI: How are you going to start your story?

Marielis doesn't remember the strategies at this point, but she does start to engage in a Maker's Talk by describing to Sarai how she started making her story by choosing the eyes for her mom's face from the loose parts. She continues talking to Sarai by pointing to all her materials and telling why she chose them.

SARAI: That's a great awesome story, Marielis!

MARIELIS: Thank you!

The two friends end their conversation with a high five and huge grins on their faces. Sarai had helped Marielis not only feel confident about what she was doing, but she also reinforced that what she had made held powerful meaning. Marielis was ready to share her story! She turned to Michelle and used her collage to tell the details of the story she had made.

Teacher tip: Capture these conversations on video to use in future lessons. Allow children to view the interaction to teach them how they can support one another during StoryMaking and share with friends.

SHARING OUR STORIES THROUGH WRITING

At first our children learned how to successfully share their stories orally during Maker's Talks. They all wanted a moment in the spotlight, and they were proud of each story they made. We then wondered, "When is it time to write, and what should the expectation be for our early learners?" We didn't want to separate writing from the Play & Make experiences they were having, as Lucy Calkins cautions, but we were already seeing their excitement to communicate through writing as they explored paper, crayons, paint, colored pencils, and other materials in the art Makerspace. We had been sharing our own stories orally, but now we wanted to show our children how to record them on paper in a fun and engaging way. Below is the focus lesson we used to introduce our children how to share by writing on new paper.

---------- STORYMAKING FOCUS LESSON ----------
Taking My Story to Paper

Objective: Children will share a story by using their documentation to help them write their story on paper.

MATERIALS

- A variety of writing paper in the writing area
- Writing tools, such as pencils and pens
- Your own story that your children have heard you play and make
- Photo or video documentation, or both, of your story with two different materials
- Familiar alphabet chart
- "How to Be a StoryMaker" anchor chart
- Documentation of children's ongoing work (pictures or actual pieces from Makerspaces)

FOCUS & EXPLORE

Connect: *"We have been working on making our stories using the different materials all around the room. You have learned how to imagine what you could make with those materials and you have returned to the same story to remake it. This is so important, because you have made your stories even better by returning to your materials again and again and adding details each time."*

Teach: *"Today I want to show you how authors take their stories to paper. After we have tried our story out with different materials, we can then write it down on paper like real authors do. Let me show you an example."*

Return to a story you have told to your children. Begin to retell the story and show children a photograph of the story with one material. Explain what you did next, such as *"Then I decided that I needed to work on my story more, so I used _____ to remake it."* Show the other photo or play video of you sharing your story with another material. Ask, *"How did I change my story?"* (Examples would be added details, made it more interesting, changed the beginning, changed the setting, added a feeling, or removed a character.)

Share both versions of the story and explain which version of the story you prefer. *"I think I like this version of the story I made, and I want to write it on paper. Watch me as I . . ."* Sing the following steps to the tune of "Shake Your Booty":

"Think, think, think." (Touch your head with finger.)

"Touch, touch, touch." (Touch the center of your paper with hand.)

"Sketch and write, sketch and write." (Signal with your hands a drawing and writing motion on the separate parts of the paper, or use sign language.)

Model sketching a picture to match your story and then add a few letters to represent the story. Use a familiar alphabet chart that the students already know well to write a letter.

Active Involvement: Review the "How to Be a StoryMaker" anchor chart with the children. Add an example of a piece of writing under the "Share" section to explain that writing is another way that we can share with others.

Documentation added to the anchor chart demonstrates the Share component of the StoryMaker Cycle.

IMAGINE

Tell children, *"Now look at our chart and think about where you are in the StoryMaker Cycle. Make a plan for your making today. Turn and tell your partner what you are going to be making today."* Share aloud a few of the children's plans and then release the students to go make. Review your anecdotal notes and check on children to see what story they are continuing.

PLAY & MAKE

Facilitate small groups who want to take their stories to paper. Prompt the children to sketch details and coach them using the alphabet chart when they are ready to add letter sounds.

SHARE

Find a student who took their story to paper and participate in a Maker's Talk with the group.

- -

When Are Children Ready to Write Their Stories?

It is important to demonstrate that all writing has a purpose and that it communicates a message whether it is in the form of scribbles or conventional writing (Hullinger-Sirken and Staley 2016). You can therefore begin modeling writing on paper during your very first cycle with StoryMaking. Use an early writing continuum to assess the developmental level of your children (drawing, scribbling, letter-like forms, letter strings, initial sounds) and model the next stage to help children easily achieve their writing goal. For example, when I first introduced writing on paper with a group of four-year-olds, I told my story out loud and then focused on the picture. Then I added a few words, but I represented the words with only a letter for each word, modeling the initial sounds. I tried to incorporate my name or the name of someone important to me, because including these names is the first meaningful writing experience for young children to have.

We also noticed that children's oral storytelling increases at a much faster rate than their writing ability. For example, children may become skilled at telling their stories using a story starter ("One sunny day . . .") followed by a series of actions ("I went outside to play on the playground with my friend Eliseo. I fell off the swings and got a cut.") and ending with a feeling ("I felt hurt."). But it can overwhelm some students to write all those words on the paper. Therefore, when a child is ready to write their story, you can ask, "Which part of your story would you like to write?" They can then choose a part and feel relaxed and confident enough to write the words on the paper ("I played.") and to let the remaining details of their story come alive in their illustration, the documentation of the made story, and the teacher dictation.

Our goal was to support our children in the writing of one page, or the beginning of their story, by the end of December. We then supported the children in the writing of two pages, which represented a beginning and the next logical event by the end of March. Finally, children were supported in the writing of three pages, which represented a beginning, middle, and end of their story, by the end of the

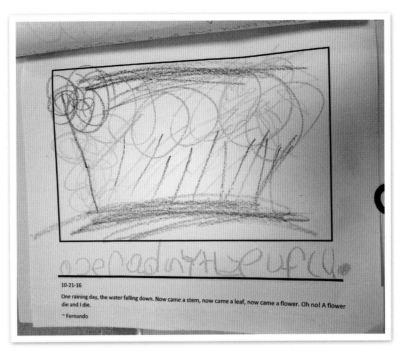

One raining day, the water falling down. Now came a stem, now came a leaf, now came a flower. Oh no! A flower die and I die.

~ Fernando

A beginning-of-the-year writing sample.

A middle-of-the-year writing sample.

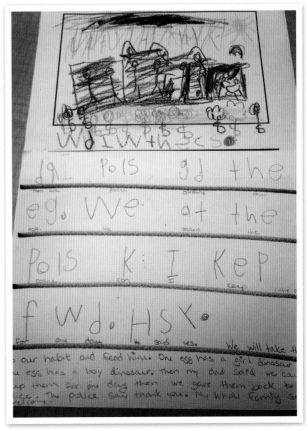

An end-of-the-year writing sample.

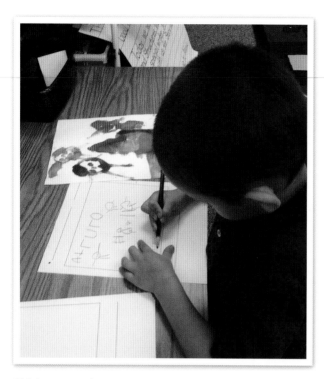

Children go to the writing Makerspace when they are ready to take their stories to paper.

school year. As noted earlier, what the students write on the page should align with an early writing continuum of development, and teachers should support children in achieving the next step through modeled and shared writing experiences throughout the year.

Not only is the learning differentiated by what the students write on the page but also in the paper we provide. It's important to think about what kind of paper the children will be writing on and where the paper will be located in the room. We recommend that you establish a writing Makerspace in your learning space where children can independently access paper and the other writing materials they may need when they want to share their stories on paper.

Lucy Calkins (2013) encourages children to write on a variety of types of paper but suggests offering only a few choices at the beginning. The paper should be different based on the child's ability to write. "You use paper to convey expectations. You assess what a child can do and channel that child to write on paper that provides the right mix of challenge and support. . . . The point is that the paper needs to march just ahead of what students can do, so that it nudges them to write more, to grow more" (42). When we first launched StoryMaking with our pre-K children, we offered two choices: a paper with only a picture box to allow children to share their story through illustrations and a paper with a picture box and one line underneath for children who were ready to write their letter-like forms or letter strings. As the children progressed through the early stages of writing, we added paper with more lines and increased the number of pages in their books.

SHARING STORIES BY PUBLISHING

One way to facilitate publishing is to select favorite stories that the children have made or written and to make books to share. But what does a published book look like for our StoryMakers? In looking through our children's StoryMaking folders, we and our teachers noticed that children had visited a variety of Makerspaces to make and remake their stories with different materials. Each piece of documentation was powerful, and we didn't want to lose the journey that children took in taking their pieces to paper, because in the maker movement, the process of making is the most important part. To honor all their hard work, we wanted to make books that would include all their documentation along with the pieces of writing.

Pages of a published book

We created the following focus lesson so that children can study a book they know well and find ways to make their published pieces special. This is a generative lesson that can be used several times to focus on making the different parts of a published book.

---------- **STORYMAKING FOCUS LESSON** ----------
How to Publish

Objective: Children will select a way to publish by studying the parts of a mentor text.

MATERIALS

- "How to Publish My Story" anchor chart
- Example of written story you modeled in the previous lesson
- Construction paper
- Markers
- Sticky notes
- Mentor text with a dust jacket you have used in another lesson

FOCUS & EXPLORE

Connect: *"We learned a few days ago that another way to share is to write our stories on paper. Many of you have been going to the writing Makerspace and getting paper to do just that. You are starting to have written stories fill up your StoryMaking folders. Now that we have shared by taking our stories to paper, we are ready for something very exciting! Are you ready?"*

Teach: *"We are going to learn how to publish our story."* Hold up the written story you modeled in a lesson prior. *"This is just a piece of paper. But one way to publish means it can go into a book."* Hold up a well-known book that the students are familiar with. *"One thing that authors do to publish their stories is to add a cover."* Show the dust jacket separately from one of the books they know. *"What we are going to do is wrap up my story!"* Place the written page inside a piece of folded white construction paper. *"This is a cover because my story is inside and my cover is outside."*

Place the blank cover on the anchor chart next to "Step 1: Wrap up my story." *"Now my cover looks very different than this author's cover, doesn't it? What did this author add to their cover that I could add?"* Allow students to study the cover and take their responses. Annotate by writing their thinking on sticky notes and placing them on the mentor text cover (illustration/picture, author's name, title). *"Wow, StoryMakers, I have some work to do on my cover."* Place the annotated mentor text cover next to the blank version on the chart.

Michelle is studying the cover with the children.

Active Involvement: Model wrapping up the story again and ask children, *"What should I add to my cover?"* Model adding a picture, title, and author's name and refer back to the written page inside to make sure it matches the story idea. After each element is created on the cover, take the sticky note off the mentor text cover and place it on yours so the children can see what they need to do next.

Completed "How to Publish My Story" anchor chart

IMAGINE

Review your anecdotal notes and check on children to see who is ready to publish. Prompt them to get their documentation out of their StoryMaking folders and go over to the table to get started designing their covers.

PLAY & MAKE

Facilitate small groups who want to take their stories to paper.

SHARE

Find a student who published to share with the group. Have the other children explain why it is a published story by referring to examples from the chart and mentor text example.

After we had taken the entire group of children through the three phases of inquiry, "Explore, Investigate, and Communicate," over the course of six to nine weeks, each child had a published piece of writing in the form of a mini-book. Children now understood the StoryMaker Cycle. They could independently imagine a material to use, and a few were imagining a story before they selected a material. They independently played and made stories every day. Some of the stories they were excited about were revisited in the following days for remaking, while other stories didn't make it to a finished product. Children have the option of placing those stories in the "all done" section of their StoryMaking folder, which allows them to abandon any story ideas. There is learning in every experience and in engaging in the StoryMaker Cycle.

• Voices from the Field •

"As I stumbled through the process, I felt a bit overwhelmed. Especially trying to listen to and dictate everyone's story and helping them take their stories to paper. I remember thinking in the beginning, "When do the kids actually write their stories?" "Shouldn't that be the main focus?" Now I realize, writing the story is probably the least important compared to all the wonderful learning opportunities StoryMaking provides. Looking back on the documentation from beginning to end, I am amazed at what the children have accomplished. They have all grown tremendously in their ability to create, share, retell, and illustrate their stories. I think what I love the most is their ability to really listen to and provide genuine compliments to their classmates. What a wonderful opportunity for them to develop positive relationships with their classmates while gaining confidence in their storytelling abilities."

—Peggy, integrated pre-K teacher

Frequency of Publishing

Once the children understood the StoryMaker Cycle and were making stories every day, we started to wonder, "How often should the children publish?" We felt that it was important during the first unit to take children through the entire inquiry framework together so they understood each part of the process. In the first unit (six to nine weeks), the students published only once. As you continue through your year, guide the children by going through the inquiry framework a few times during subsequent units. In the chart below, you will see how we used mini-inquiry cycles of about two to three weeks each to move children through the phases several times in units two through four. This increased the amount of publishing the students produced. For example, select a few Phase 1 lessons, move on to remaking and investigating how to make the stories better in Phase 2 lessons, and then at the end of the mini-inquiry cycle, have students choose a way to publish. Then repeat by returning to Phase 1 to introduce a new material, and so on. By increasing the rate at which you teach each phase, you will give your children more opportunities to share, write, and publish their stories throughout the year.

──────────────── **Phase 1** ────────────────
(approximately 1 to 2 weeks)

Focus Lesson Examples:

1. Introduce a mentor text connected to unit (e.g., in our "structures" unit we introduced *Building a House* to imagine how we could develop story ideas using photographs.)
2. Sketch a favorite place, object, or memory to imagine new ideas connected to the unit
3. Teach a planning strategy before the children play and make (e.g., brainstorm settings by adding the "Where" to the ongoing anchor chart.)
4. Introduce new materials to make a story (e.g., bamboo houses and then the sand area)
5. Introduce one new way to start a story (e.g., start by describing the setting using *Building a House* by Byron Barton.)

──────── **Phase 3** ────────
(approximately a few days to a week)

Focus Lesson Examples:

1. Take the story to paper using documentation and the alphabet chart (work with students in small groups)
2. Prompt a new way to share
3. Publish
4. Have a mini-celebration

──────── **Phase 2** ────────
(approximately 1 week)

Focus Lesson Examples:

1. Revise the story by choosing a different material
2. Do an illustration study with setting details (a few days)
3. Write letters or labels for the illustration (model how to form letters)

Publishing Can Include Other "Languages"

Writing or making a book is only one way to publish. In order for all children to have access to StoryMaking, we must broaden our understanding of what it can mean to publish a story. It could include an oral retelling of course, but we would like to encourage the use of the other Hundred Languages as a way to publish. Children should have variety when sharing their stories. Here are some examples of what we imagine publishing to look like, and we invite you to grow the list with your own powerful ideas:

- Children can display an image, sculpture, or other representation of their story with materials they used for an audience to view.

- Children can use the props they used to make their story and act out the story for an audience.

- Children can select music and perform a dance to convey the actions and feelings of their characters in the story.

- Children can play a video of themselves making their story for an audience to view.

- Children can use technology to create a slide show or movie to share their story.

We continue to broaden our view of how children can go public and communicate their stories to an audience. Kristin Rainville and Bill Gordh (2016) describe the use of technology as another powerful way to share our stories and affirm the enormous role digital storytelling plays in our twenty-first-century life. They also tell about a process that supported a collaborative storytelling experience: Children told stories orally as a group by passing around a wooden turtle. As the turtle was handed to each child, they added another detail to the story. In the following days, the teacher replaced the turtle with images on an iPad showing the wooden turtle in different positions. The children returned to this turtle story and "tried on" different versions to repurpose their ideas by narrating the actions of the turtle. Rainville and Gordh suggest that you can take still photos and allow the children to narrate their own images to create the class story. These images can then be placed into iMovie, and the children can watch their narrated slide show, which demonstrates yet another way to publish. We decided to give it a try with our Makerspaces and as a collaborative group.

One class of our pre-K children had been working together to build tents out of sticks, netting, and other found materials in their outdoor classroom and play area. Ms. Rachel, the pre-K teacher, had taken photographs of each part of their making process and then guided them into creating a story using these images. Here is an example of their digital storytelling experience and published story:

Children play and make a collaborative story with found materials.

"One day we went to the park and built a fort. We played in it. Then we went home. We had a campfire. We had friends come to the campfire. We had fun!"

WE MUST CELEBRATE!

Finally, it is important to end a unit with some kind of celebration. This is a time to celebrate everything the children have learned as StoryMakers and to keep their motivation going to continue to make more stories. Many teachers make the learning environment extra special by placing tablecloths on their tables, sharing a snack together, and inviting special people to hear or view the children's stories. There are endless possibilities for taking time to honor the hard work your StoryMakers have accomplished, but the most important thing is that you take time to reflect and celebrate with your children. Here are some ideas for celebrations:

- Invite parents or another class, or even have the students bring in their favorite stuffed animal, for them to retell their stories to, while everyone enjoys snacks.

- Invite parents, other classrooms, and volunteers to hear the stories the children have written in small group circles. Allow children to use their materials as well to show their story.

- Create a display of their year of learning and host a museum walk. Children may walk around the published stories and leave comments and compliments on sticky notes by one another's work.

- Create a documentation board to hang the published work and invite the school community into the celebration as well.

Ms. Shannon's children hang their first published works in the hallway.

TIPS FOR STUDENTS WITH SPECIAL RIGHTS

To make this lesson accessible to all early learners, we recommend the following tips:

- Videotape the child making their story, and play the video during a Maker's Talk. Afterward, retell the actions they viewed in the video. Ask children to describe what they viewed their friend doing in the video so the child can see that their actions hold meaning and that they are making a story through play.

- Display photos of the child making their story and allow them to put the photos in order of what happened in the story.

- Provide physical props for children to re-enact their story.

WHAT TO EXPECT DURING PHASE 3 OF YOUR FIRST UNIT

During Phase 3, "Communicate," of our StoryMaking units, children are guided to select a story they want to go public with and share with a chosen audience. The goal of this phase is for the children to choose a way to share what they have made and to celebrate their new StoryMaking skills. We encourage them to use any of the "languages" from the Reggio approach. Below is a list to highlight the educator roles and observed behaviors from our children that you may expect during implementation.

The goals of the StoryMaking focus lessons may include the following:

- Help share a story. You may want to watch videos of students asking each other questions about their creations.

- Demonstrate how to wrap up a story by selecting a story and wrapping it up with a cover.

- Study a mentor text to see what else makes a published story.

- Create a special section in the classroom library for published works.

- Celebrate with one another on all you have learned as StoryMakers.

Below are your roles during Phase 3:

- Familiarize yourself with StoryMaking learning progressions to establish goals for students and class.

Here are the child behaviors you may observe during Play & Make:

- Children will continue to use pictures and videos to share their story or rebuild it using materials.

- Children will write according to their ability on one piece of paper. It will include at least one picture of the material used to make their story.

- Children may have difficulty describing what makes a published story using a mentor text because they are focused on retelling the story of that book.

- Children develop agency and character when publishing a story and sharing with others.

- Children begin to truly see themselves as a StoryMakers and authors!

FINAL THOUGHTS

When children have retold their story using different materials, they may choose to take their story to paper—an important step for teachers to observe as students' progress in this area of their emergent literacy skills. Even so, we want children to understand that there are many ways to share their stories that will tap into their strengths and allow them to fully express what they have learned. Remember to encourage both individual and collaborative stories and to take time to celebrate the learning. We look forward to celebrating with you after you complete your first cycle of the StoryMaking process. We hope you communicate the stories you make and lessons you've learned so we can all continue to grow from one another's experiences in our new community of StoryMakers!

Maker's Moment

Here is a documentation story of an ESOL student who entered our classrooms with very little English language. He did not speak at the beginning of the year but understood the StoryMaking process. By observing him during his play and recording his actions, we could interpret that he was telling some creative stories. Here is Juan sharing and using his props from the water table to communicate his story just a few months into our StoryMaking routine. Michelle narrated his actions and Juan provided the words in bold:

Juan is sharing his story.

*"One day there were **two** sharks. They were **eating fish** because they were so hungry. They felt **better**. Their bellies were full, so they went to **sleep**."*

The Role of Documentation

DOCUMENTATION CREATES OPPORTUNITIES FOR CHILDREN AND TEACHERS

Teachers are never without a clipboard, a sticky note, a camera, a pencil, or an electronic device. They listen and watch. They observe such things as what materials the students find engaging, what tools they use with fluency, and how the children communicate with one another. They record what the children are doing and saying and how they are interacting. They record the children's story renditions, their thinking along the way, and the processes and materials they use to make their stories. They use the recorded information to determine next steps along the learning continuums. It is hard work. It takes time to learn.

Whenever I walk into Ms. Shannon's classroom, she is sitting with the children, either in the block Makerspace, or at housekeeping, or in collage. She is surrounded by children. They often don't notice her, as they are used to her sitting and watching and taking notes while asking occasional questions to gather additional information, get clarification, or understand what the children are thinking. Ms. Shannon's paraprofessional, Ms. Dina, is also always working with the children, recording their stories, taking photos of their stories, or watching and listening. Ms. Shannon had noticed the children were spending most of their time in collage. She made it her goal that week to pay attention and to record the materials in collage her children were the most engaged with throughout the week. Once Ms. Shannon had gathered evidence on how often they were using the same materials to build their stories, she figured out which materials were the children's favorites. She made notes on her interpretations of how to support their making in other areas in the room. She strategically placed the children's favorite materials in new Makerspaces, thus provoking new curiosity and interest in underused spaces.

Ms. Shannon has a notebook that includes information about story topics, materials used to make stories, and where the children are in the process of building their stories. She did not start out on day one of StoryMaking knowing how to

Michelle records stories in Ms. Shannon's room as the children are making in the attachments Makerspace.

document. She began slowly, first by taking pictures when the children told her they had made a story, then by observing them more closely and making little notes to herself on sticky notes, recording the ideas the children had come up with for their stories. In time, and with the development of some of the tools we'll share with you, Ms. Shannon came to regularly record the children's material uses and ideas that would help her interpret their learning and determine next steps.

StoryMaking offers the perfect opportunity to share a common experience, demonstrate learning, and determine what comes next. Observing children and noticing what Makerspaces they enjoy most, which materials inspire them, and what topics they gravitate toward is the beginning of documentation. As the children make their stories, you can capture their ideas and processes with photos or video, which can be used as a reminder to you and the children of what stories they are making. Documentation provides an opportunity for you to be the StoryMaker, by making stories about a particular child's learning growth, favorite spaces, and shared experiences.

WHAT IS DOCUMENTATION?

There are many types of assessment. In our state we have a mandated VPK (Voluntary Prekindergarten) assessment that is standardized and administered three times a year. We are required to administer this assessment, but we also employ authentic assessment processes in our classrooms. Documentation provides a way to make students' thinking and learning visible. It enables us to observe and follow the children's interests and questions; to collect data on their learning; to make informed instructional decisions; and to share with families what we're learning. Documentation has also provided many opportunities for our teachers to collaborate with one another, learn more about themselves as teachers and researchers, and improve their teaching practices.

There are several different definitions of documentation, but we tend toward Susan Stacey's definition that documentation is "the practice of making children's and teachers' thinking and learning visible through graphic displays of photography, work samples, and text" (2015, ix). If we don't know what children are thinking, then it is difficult to monitor their learning and develop relevant and meaningful next steps to move their learning forward.

LEARNING TO DOCUMENT

Many of you who work with young children already document a number of things in your classrooms using a variety of tools (assessment scores, student portfolios, literacy checklists, job assignments, attendance records), so learning to document during StoryMaking will be a natural part of your practice. For others, this will be a beginning. Let's get started!

Learning the craft of documentation takes time. It is a process and doesn't happen overnight. Teachers typically go through stages along a developmental continuum when they learn to document. Hilary Seitz, in "The Power of Documentation in the Early Childhood Classroom" (2008), names each of the stages. We have added to her descriptions, using both Susan Stacey's suppositions and our teachers' experiences. These stages are similar to a learning progression, showing each step along the way toward proficiency of a standard or goal. The object is to identify where you fit in with your knowledge along the continuum and to look ahead at next steps to figure out where you need to go next. This section details the practical application of documentation to StoryMaking and the how-to steps that fall along the continuum.

This process is not a race, and no one expects you to move through the stages quickly. Go at your own pace and know that documenting your students' work, learning, and progress will make StoryMaking even better.

First Steps

Beginning Documentation
An initial mistake teachers make is trying to document *everything*. This can be overwhelming, so take it one step at a time. Even if, in the beginning, you simply post

pictures of student work on a bulletin board or write students' comments about a particular event, then it will show the students that you believe their work and their words are important. The authors of *Maker-Centered Learning* state, "The more visible tools, materials, and student work are, the more likely it is that students will make new connections" (Clapp et al. 2017, 45).

Susan Stacey, in *Pedagogical Documentation in Early Childhood* (2015), suggests starting with observing children playing and interacting with one another and with their materials, and thinking of a question that you have with regard to what the children are learning or how they're learning. She cautions that you start by focusing on only one question, and keep notes and photographs that pertain specifically to the one question you're investigating. Some questions that we started out with include, "What materials in the Makerspace are the most engaging for the children?" "How did our nature walk inspire stories?" "What are some options I see students using for beginning their stories that I can highlight during a focus lesson?"

An example of the beginnings of documentation used in Ms. Angela's room, in which she took dictation in the collage Makerspace.

Exploring Technology

This step includes figuring out what device to use to take pictures or video, and how to photograph, download pictures, save them in electronic files, and print them. Photographs and video are helpful only when they get used. For some, this step is natural, and many teachers are already masters at using and manipulating technology. For others, this will be a difficult step in the process. Many of our teachers use their cell phones. Check to make sure that you're allowed to record on your personal devices in your state. We also ordered iPad minis for our teachers. Some use their computers for photos and recordings. It is not mandatory that you start with or use technology. It can simply be a step in the process. As an alternative to technology, our teachers have developed some documents on which they record individual student's dictations and conversations, glue actual photographs, or draw illustrations that provide details about students' stories.

The most important thing is for you to develop an organized system that makes sense for you in your classroom. Some teachers work from a device, while others have clipboards placed around the classroom. Still others post sticky notes everywhere and grab one when they need it. If our documentation forms (in the appendix) prove helpful to you, then feel free to use them or revise them to meet your needs.

Next Steps

These next stages offer practical information and tips about how to apply the practices of documentation in a realistic way. The framework offered by Mara Krechevsky, Ben Mardell, Melissa Rivard, and Daniel Wilson (2013) is very helpful to outline the basic steps of documentation. We frame our discussion with our teachers' suggestions. Krechevsky et al. "suggest four core practices of documentation that teachers, students, and others can engage in across contexts to support and communicate learning. They are observing, recording, interpreting, and sharing" (77). We will detail each of these practices within the context of StoryMaking and describe how each practice lends itself to assessment of student learning.

Observing

This is the stage at which the documenter (you!) can focus on the purpose of documenting. When you align documentation with the inquiry cycle, observation is Phase 1. It requires that you watch and listen to see what is going on with your students. Who is doing what? With whom? Why? How? It is the mucking-about part of assessment. It means checking in with yourself to see if what you thought was happening with student engagement and learning is actually happening.

Although the task of observation sounds easy, for a teacher to stop and simply watch is difficult. Working with young children, you are so used to multitasking, being productive, and never slowing down that when you're observing the students, it can feel like you're not getting anything done. Even though it feels as if you're not accomplishing anything, you are really doing important work as you attend to your students, their actions, engagements, feelings, interactions, and conversations. The most productive observations occur when teachers are open to the possibilities of seeing their own and their students' misconceptions, experiencing unanticipated outcomes, and noticing surprises in students' understandings and engagements.

A difficulty some of our teachers experienced when they first started document-ing was in determining what they were supposed to observe and document. Mara Krechevsky et al., like Susan Stacey, suggest that "formulating a question helps focus and limit data collection and sharpens analysis" (2013, 78). Julianne Wurm, on the other hand, says, "the simplest way to begin may be to choose a time of day or area of the classroom to observe for a week or two or even three" (2005, 104).

If you don't already have a question you want to focus your observation on, then you may choose an event, a child, or a space on which to focus the observation. During StoryMaking, the children use their imaginations, play, make, and share their stories. Teachers can naturally focus on any one of these components of the StoryMaker Cycle. Other possibilities for productive observations could include the children's use of materials, particular story components, their writings, stu-dents' interactions with one another, or their proficiency in building complex stories. Because teachers carefully consider their choices in the lessons they plan for inspiration, and because students are naturally curious about new materials and experiences, children are typically engaged during StoryMaking. It is up to the teacher to determine which components of this engagement to record and reflect on.

Some examples of the components for documentation our teachers have focused on include an event, a child, or a space. One teacher documented an event near one of our sites—the work of a construction crew. The children were intrigued. The teacher decided to take a walk and let the children watch the construction pro-cess for a bit. She documented the children's comments while they were watching. Then, when they returned to their room, they discussed the children's thinking. They made a chart and discussed jobs, hard hats, construction, trucks, cranes. This led to all sorts of stories, and the teacher could refer back to her documentation when children got stuck or lost interest. She determined that her children were most interested in the machinery, and it led to many inquiries on machinery used in the construction industry, accompanied by many stories.

Recording

StoryMaking offers ideal opportunities to take anecdotal notes, write transcriptions of children's conversations and storytelling, and photograph or draw the selection and uses of materials to show how the materials were used to make the children's stories and grow their learning. The records can be used the next day for reference and reflection as children hack and repurpose their stories. Students add details and emotions and extend their stories when they have a reminder of their story in the form of a photograph, video, or transcription. These records can also be used as concrete exemplars or as highlights for inspiration; during share time to scaffold the students as they go public with their stories; and as a piece of an entire story or display of the process of learning as the children engage in making a story.

Wurm, in *Working in the Reggio Way* (2005), describes the recording of a chronological process of what happened in a selected work project. This suggestion aligns with recording the chronological processes of StoryMaking and, in particular, the StoryMaking of a specific child. Our teachers use notebooks for their documentation and arrange everything chronologically and according to individual children's names. Documenters may start to add text to photographs, write dictations of stories, and take anecdotal notes of their observations, thoughts, and reflections.

We've developed three documentation forms that our teachers use regularly to record their children's StoryMaking. Copies of these forms are provided in the appendix. Below is a description of each form along with an example of one filled out.

Status of Stories. We first suggest beginning documentation using our Status of Stories Documentation Record. This form allows you to record the material (playdough), Makerspace (collage), and/or story idea (family goes to the park) for each child in the class on one form. This form is used during the "Imagine" part of the focus lesson and allows the educator to interpret patterns by looking at what each child has imagined over the course of a week. Codes and highlighting can also be used so you can keep track of how often you conference with individual students as well as select students for the share portion of StoryMaking.

The Status of Stories Documentation Record allows for tracking stories for an entire class.

Student Name	ML–Collage Date: 9/9	Play-doh Date: 9/16	Remake Date: 9/22	Watercolors Date: 10/27	Who, what, feeling Date: 12/1	
Anycia	Collage ✓ Dog @ beach	Housekeeping Me & Michelle Story ★	play doh need to imagine	Collage fish died sad	Blue playdoh Dad hurt sick	
Juan	Blocks need to imagine story	Collage ✓ need to imagine	Blocks ✓ fish ate frogs	water tub ✓ 2 sharks eating ★	Blue playdoh eating cake happy ✓	
Audrey	Blocks Dog story	Blocks Monster story	Art ✓ remake dog story ★	water tub beach story	Art then blocks ★ remake beach ✓	
Alison	Collage ✓ princess story	Play-doh froggie story	Collage ✓ making a pond ★	Collage adding more details	pink playdoh dog scratching excited ✓	

☑ Conference
★ Share
Status of Stories Documentation Record
Class At-A-Glance

StoryMaking Documentation Record. After you are comfortable documenting this basic information, you can become more detailed in your recording practices. When meeting with individual children during Play & Make time, we encourage you to take dictation of the stories children are telling. The StoryMaking Documentation Record allows the teacher to record the story only and provides space for documenting three conferences over time. Write the material the children used to make their story and any explanation of their story prior to sharing it. Then write down exactly what the child says in the dictation portion of the form to document their story. You may ask the child what they want to work on as a StoryMaker next and write that in the "Writing Goal" section. This is also an area the educator can use to jot down the next steps they think the child may need for further instruction.

The StoryMaking Documentation Record helps in recording stories and next steps for an individual child.

StoryMaking Photo Documentation Record. The StoryMaking Photo Documentation Record allows the educator to fully implement documentation practices by not only recording the story children have made and shared with you but also including photo documentation of the story they have made. It includes all the same information as the StoryMaking Documentation Record but allows you to attach pictures you've taken of the story the child has made with the chosen material.

The StoryMaking Photo Documentation Record includes photos along with a child's stories.

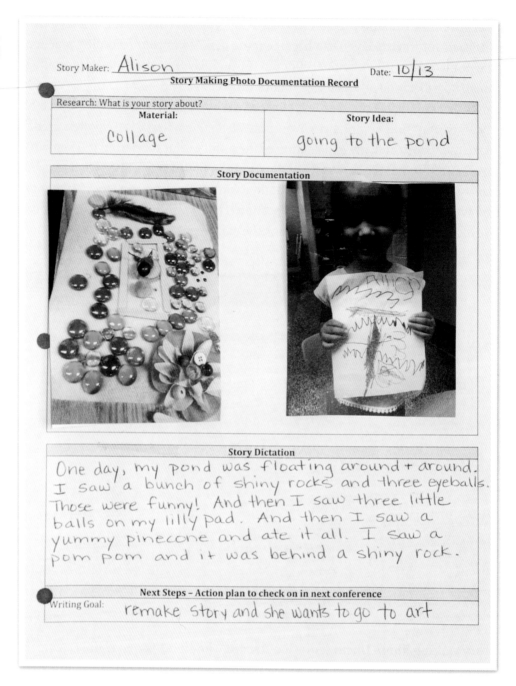

Story Maker: **Alison**   Date: **10/13**

Story Making Photo Documentation Record

Research: What is your story about?

Material:	Story Idea:
Collage	going to the pond

Story Documentation

Story Dictation

One day, my pond was floating around + around. I saw a bunch of shiny rocks and three eyeballs. Those were funny! And then I saw three little balls on my lilly pad. And then I saw a yummy pinecone and ate it all. I saw a pom pom and it was behind a shiny rock.

Next Steps – Action plan to check on in next conference

Writing Goal: remake story and she wants to go to art

To plan whole group focus lessons, we recommend you have a Status of Stories Documentation Record for the class. Then select either of the individual documentation forms so you can record each child's StoryMaking progression over time.

To make your focus lessons more relevant and engaging, record students' making processes, partial stories, materials, and final products. Use these documentation samples during your focus lessons as examples. The children love to see their work and respond positively to their friends' StoryMaking efforts. This is also a way that all children's efforts and unique stories can be celebrated.

Interpreting

Thus far, by observing and recording, we have enough information to make a beautiful display, but for documentation to be meaningful, it must be interpreted. Something has to be done with the artifacts and observations to ensure students' learning continues to grow. Susan Stacey refers to this as "conceptualizing the purpose of documentation . . . making learning visible" (2015, 20). Interpreting is not easy. It takes attention, time, and expertise. Interpretation is easier when worked on collaboratively with colleagues and friends as others can view your documentation through a different lens, offer new and different ideas, and provide a variety of areas of expertise and experience that can help you recognize needs and move student learning forward.

Robin and Ms. Rachel review documentation to interpret what the children have learned.

Often, when we are "in the moment," we may view an event or experience differently than when we reflect on it later. Documentation can serve to disrupt what we thought was happening and serve as evidence of what really has happened. Interpreting our observations and recordings can illuminate what learners have learned, what learners can do, and where they are on a learning continuum so that we can determine next steps along the developmental progressions. The process of interpretation enables teachers to have professional conversations about instructional decisions; grounds the discussions in a child's work and data; and serves as a platform for professional development and learning. This process is what makes documentation valuable for moving both the adult's and the children's learning forward.

Observations and recordings provide evidence for interpretations of a child's learning. A simple statement like "You have been playing with blocks and making your story for three days. What new space would you like to make your story in today?" demonstrates that the teacher has been noticing a child's actions and has decided the child needs to try out the story in a new space. Another example is seen in this teacher's comment: "I was looking at my documentation today, and I've noticed that you have not started on a new story lately. As you are playing, what materials will help you begin to imagine a story?" Interpretation of documentation proves helpful when children are stuck in a particular space, material, topic, or story. Interpreting your documentation can help you move the children's Story-Making forward.

Sharing

Depending on the purpose of your documentation, you may choose to share your StoryMaking documentation with the students, families, and other teachers.

Children. Documentation can be shared in many ways with the children during StoryMaking each day:

- Use photos or videos of students' stories or materials to help you make a teaching point during a focus lesson.

- Post photographs of students' uses of materials in each of the Maker-spaces to show proper uses of materials or to provide ideas of how the children can use the materials to make their stories.

Ms. Angela shows Steven his documentation to discuss which parts he wants to remake in his fish story.

- Use your documentation to scaffold the children as they share their stories each day. Children who participate in Maker's Talks can use photographs and recordings of their StoryMaking to help them remember their stories and give them visual cues.

- Use your documentation of individual student's learning to discuss with them how much they've learned, a particular area you want them to work on, or new ways to stretch their learning. For example, one of our teachers, Sally, referred to documentation when discussing how to generate new StoryMaking ideas with a student: "Ariel, I notice in these pictures that your last three settings have all been in castles. Would you like to look in these books to get some new ideas about other settings you could use in your stories?"

Families. Sharing is also a special time to include the families. If you document StoryMaking along the way, then families are informed throughout a unit about students' stories, learning, and curiosities. This provides conversation starters for families, enables families to better support the learning going on in the classroom, and creates an inclusive culture of StoryMaking in which families play a vital role. It is always wonderful to include families as part of the learning community, and documentation offers a great way to keep families connected to the learning and events in the classroom. Our teachers often post documentation stories in the hallway so that families can see it when they bring the children to school. There is also an app called Kaymbu that is easy to use and keeps parents updated and informed each day. If you prefer digital communication, then this could be a good option for you.

Other Teachers. Sharing your documentation with other teachers can provide you with expertise and fresh perspectives for interpreting your documentation. A professional learning community can be an ideal setting for sharing your documentation, thinking, interpretation, and ideas for next steps in instruction during Story-Making with others.

Teachers record their interpretations to discuss and share during professional learning communities.

Final Steps

"Documenters combine work samples, photographs, descriptions, and miscellaneous information in support of the entire learning event. They tell the whole story with a beginning, middle, and an end, using supporting artifacts" (Seitz 2008, 92). This "whole" story could be several iterations of StoryMaking by one child who grows the stories across a variety of materials and creates a final published work example or shares one particular story. Or it could be a gathering of each story made by a child over time, comparing the growth in oral language, materials' uses, or other literacies enacted during StoryMaking. It could be a study of the progress of the entire class across the social-emotional domain and the collaborative stories built during StoryMaking—whatever individual or collaborative stories come to the fore in your room that might reflect student learning.

Ideally, both adults and children will document. In a classroom where documentation is a practice, students see teachers model and use documentation to revisit, reflect on, and move learning forward. Students see value in their work and can easily learn to take their own pictures or draw renditions of their stories each day. The steps discussed for teachers' documentation earlier (observing, recording, interpreting, and sharing) are the same steps students can be taught to attend to as they learn to document. Students have fun photographing the StoryMaking materials, processes, and final product; recording their going public during share time; and sharing their documentation with their families and learning community.

TIPS FOR STUDENTS WITH SPECIAL RIGHTS

> **• Voices from the Field •**
>
> *What is your favorite part of StoryMaking?*
>
> "Seeing the kids blossom with it—because their creativity excels anything that I could come up with. Sometimes I have to let go of modeling it myself and let them model it because they have more brilliant ideas than I do."
>
> —Tara, integrated pre-K teacher

StoryMaking can honor all children's multimodal literacies (signing, dancing, singing, building, weaving), and so does documentation. All students can use photographs of their work in some way. They may simply be excited to recognize themselves, may be able to use the photo as the background for building another story, or may claim something as theirs. All children have stories to tell, but it's up to us to capture them. StoryMaking honors all stories, regardless of materials, complexity, or speed. As children build their stories, they come to know themselves and their worlds a little better.

- You may want to label some photographs with words or vocabulary that represent what the children want to convey. You could even write right on the photo if that would serve as a reminder of the story or event. The photograph could become a page in the StoryMaking process, an opportunity to grow vocabulary, or a reflection of the child as a StoryMaker!

- Take pictures of students as they play in chronological steps to give them an opportunity to share. They can point, sign, and act out to share their story, with the documentation as their guide.

- Documentation is the same for all students. It starts with observation. As you observe students with language difficulties or other needs, observe what they like. Where do they go? How do they engage with materials? Capture them with photos while playing. If they don't know how to play, create some focus lessons that model play behaviors. You can use the pictures and narrate what they are doing in the photos, if they are nonverbal. Have them point as you are describing the actions and materials.

FINAL THOUGHTS

Learning to document is a process and takes time, but it will serve you well as you begin to develop expertise and use your documentation to measure learning in a variety of domains; note areas of student interest, engagement, or need; and move learning forward. We hope that reading this chapter gave you some ideas about how you can begin to grow your documentation expertise. Start with something that feels comfortable to your teaching style and that enables you to capture and celebrate children's stories, learning, and lives.

Maker's Moment

At the beginning of the year, Ms. Lori and her paraprofessional invited the children to share their stories. They quickly dictated their stories on blank paper so the children could have the words with their material.

Ms. Lori records Elijah's story on paper.

Then several months into StoryMaking, Ms. Lori began to take pictures and videotape the children sharing their stories. She began using technology to record the play, make, and share process. Here is Emily's story that she recorded:

(continued)

Ms. Lori videotapes Emily as she shares her story.

"The pig was outside and he slipped! And he fell down."

At the end of the year, Ms. Lori was a pro at documentation. She set up OneDrive folders, then scanned and uploaded photos and writing for each of her children. Here is the recorded story of one of her four-year-olds, Jayson:

A sample of Jayson's scanned spider story.

Appendix

Status of Stories Documentation Record
Class At-a-Glance

Student Name	Date:	Date:	Date:	Date:	Date:

StoryMaking Documentation Record

StoryMaker: _____ **Date:** _____

Research _What is your story about?_	Story Dictation _Notes of student's oral storytelling_	Next Steps _Action plan to check on in next conference_
Material: Story Idea:		StoryMaking Goal:

StoryMaker: _____ **Date:** _____

Research _What is your story about?_	Story Dictation _Notes of student's oral storytelling_	Next Steps _Action plan to check on in next conference_
Material: Story Idea:		StoryMaking Goal:

StoryMaker: _____ **Date:** _____

Research _What is your story about?_	Story Dictation _Notes of student's oral storytelling_	Next Steps _Action plan to check on in next conference_
Material: Story Idea:		StoryMaking Goal:

StoryMaking Photo Documentation Record

StoryMaker: _____ **Date:** _____

Research: What is your story about?	
Material:	Story Idea:

Story Documentation

Story Dictation

Next Steps: Action plan to check on at next conference
StoryMaking Goal:

References

Barell, John. 2013. *Did You Ever Wonder: Fostering Curiosity Here, There and Everywhere.* Berwick-upon-Tweed, UK: Martins the Printers Ltd.

———. 2015. *Problem-Based Learning: An Inquiry Approach.* Thousand Oaks, CA: Corwin.

Brahms, Lisa, and Kevin Crowley. 2016. "Making Sense of Making: Defining Learning Practices in MAKE Magazine." In *Makeology: Makers as Learners,* vol. 2, edited by Kylie Peppler, Erica Rosenfeld Halverson, and Yasmin B. Kafai, 13–28. New York: Routledge.

Brahms, Lisa, and Peter Wardrip. 2016. "Making with Young Learners: An Introduction." *Teaching Young Children* 9 (5). www.naeyc.org/tyc/making-young-learners-intro.

———. 2017. "The What, How, and Why of Making." *Teaching Young Children* 10 (3): 16–17.

Calkins, Lucy. 1994. *The Art of Teaching Writing.* Portsmouth, NH: Heinemann.

———. 2001. *The Art of Teaching Reading.* Portsmouth, NH: Heinemann.

———. 2013. *A Guide to the Common Core Writing Workshop: Primary Grades.* Portsmouth, NH: Heinemann.

Chalufour, Ingrid, and Karen Worth. 2003. *Discovering Nature with Young Children.* The Young Scientist Series. St. Paul, MN: Redleaf Press.

Christakis, Erika. 2016. *The Importance of Being Little: What Preschoolers Really Need from Grownups.* New York: Viking.

Clapp, Edward, Jessica Ross, Jennifer Ryan, and Shari Tishman. 2017. *Maker-Centered Learning: Empowering Young People to Shape Their Worlds.* San Francisco: Jossey-Bass.

Clay, Marie. 2000. *Concepts About Print: What Have Children Learned about Printed Language?* Portsmouth, NH: Heinemann.

Davidson, Simon. 2009. "Communities of Inquiry." In *International Perspectives on Inquiry Learning,* edited by Steven Carber and Simon Davidson, 27–42. London, UK: John Catt.

Dorfman, Lynne, and Rose Cappelli. 2007. *Mentor Texts: Teaching Writing through Children's Literature, K–6.* Portland, ME: Stenhouse.

Edwards, Carolyn, Lella Gandini, and George Forman, eds. 1998. *The Hundred Languages of Children: The Reggio Emilia Approach—Advanced Reflections.* 2nd ed. Greenwich, CT: Ablex Publishing.

Fields, Deborah, and Victor Lee. 2016. "Craft Technologies 101: Bringing Making to Higher Education." In *Makeology: Makerspaces as Learning Environments,* vol. 1, edited by Kylie Peppler, Erica Rosenfeld Halverson, and Yasmin B. Kafai, 121–38. New York: Routledge.

Fleming, Laura. 2015. *Worlds of Making, Best Practices for Establishing a Makerspace for Your School.* Corwin Connected Educators Series. Thousand Oaks, CA: Corwin Press.

Flewitt, Rosie. 2013. "Multimodal Perspectives on Early Childhood Literacies." In *Handbook of Early Childhood Literacy,* edited by Joanne Larson and Jackie Marsh, 295–309. London: Sage.

Gauntlett, David, and Bo Stjerne Thomsen. 2013. *Cultures of Creativity: Nurturing Creative Mindsets across Cultures.* The LEGO Foundation. www.legofoundation.com/it-it/research-and-learning/foundation-research/cultures-creativity.

Glover, Matt. 2009. *Engaging Young Writers: Preschool–Grade 1.* Portsmouth, NH: Heinemann.

Gopnik, Alison. 2010. "A Conversation with Dr. Alison Gopnik." *Teaching Young Children* 3 (2): 26–27.

Hamlin, Maria, and Debora Wisneski. 2012. "Supporting the Scientific Thinking and Inquiry of Toddlers and Preschoolers through Play." *Young Children* 67 (3): 82–88.

Harvey, Stephanie, and Harvey Daniels. 2009. *Comprehension and Collaboration: Inquiry Circles in Action*. Portsmouth, NH: Heinemann.

Heard, Georgia, and Jennifer McDonough. 2009. *A Place for Wonder: Reading and Writing Nonfiction in the Primary Grades*. Portland, ME: Stenhouse Publishers.

Heroman, Cate. 2017. *Making and Tinkering with STEM: Solving Design Challenges with Young Children*. Washington, DC: National Association for the Education of Young Children.

Honig, Alice. 2007. "Oral Language Development." *Early Childhood Development and Care* 177 (6/7): 581–613.

Hullinger-Sirken, Holly, and Lynn Staley. 2016. "Teacher Inquiry on the Influence of Materials on Children's Learning." *Young Children* 71 (5): 64–73.

Katz, Lilian. 1998. "What Can We Learn from Reggio Emilia?" In *The Hundred Languages of Children*, 2nd ed., edited by Carolyn Edwards, Lella Gandini, and George Forman, 27–45. Greenwich, CT: Ablex Publishing.

Krechevsky, Mara, Ben Mardell, Melissa Rivard, and Daniel Wilson. 2013. *Visible Learners: Promoting Reggio-Inspired Approaches in All Schools*. San Francisco: Jossey Bass.

Kress, Gunther. 2013. "Perspectives on Making Meaning: The Differential Principles and Means of Adults and Children." In *Handbook of Early Childhood Literacy*, edited by Joanne Larson and Jackie Marsh, 329–44. London: Sage.

Lewis, Sarah. 2014. *The Rise: Creativity, the Gift of Failure, and the Search for Mastery*. New York: Simon & Schuster.

MacKay, Susan. 2013. *Equity and Access through Story Workshop: Supporting Inclusion for Children with Disabilities by Developing Connections between the Arts and Literacy*. Portland, OR: Portland Children's Museum.

Malaguzzi, Loris. 1998. "History, Ideas, and Basic Philosophy: An Interview with Lella Gandini. In *The Hundred Languages of Children: The Reggio Emilia Approach—Advanced Reflections*, 2nd ed., edited by Carolyn Edwards, Lella Gandini, and George Forman, 49–97. Greenwich, CT: Ablex Publishing.

McGalliard, Mike. 2016. "From a Movie to a Movement: Caine's Arcade and the Imagination Foundation. In *Makeology: Makers as Learners*, vol. 2, edited by Kylie Peppler, Erica Rosenfeld Halverson, and Yasmin B. Kafai, 111–24. New York: Routledge.

Mraz, Kristine, and Christine Hertz. 2015. *A Mindset for Learning: Teaching the Traits of Joyful, Independent Growth*. Portsmouth, NH: Heinemann.

Mraz, Kristine, Alison Porcelli, and Cheryl Tyler. 2016. *Purposeful Play: A Teacher's Guide to Igniting Deep and Joyful Learning across the Day*. Portsmouth, NH: Heinemann.

NAEYC (National Association for the Education of Young Children). 2009. *Developmentally Appropriate Practice in Early Childhood Programs Serving Children from Birth through Age 8*. A Position Statement. www.naeyc.org/files/naeyc/file/positions/PSDAP.pdf.

Pelo, Ann. 2017. *The Language of Art: Inquiry-Based Studio Practices in Early Childhood Settings*. 2nd ed. St. Paul, MN: Redleaf Press.

Pinnell, Gay, and Irene Fountas. 2011. *Literacy Beginnings: A Prekindergarten Handbook*. Portsmouth, NH: Heinemann.

Rainville, Kristin, and Bill Gordh. 2016. "Toward a Narrative Classroom: Storytelling, Media, and Literacy." *Young Children* 71 (4): 76–81.

Ray, Katie Wood. 2010. *In Pictures and In Words: Teaching the Qualities of Good Writing through Illustration Study.* Portsmouth, NH: Heinemann.

Ray, Katie Wood, and Matt Glover. 2008. *Already Ready: Nurturing Writers in Preschool and Kindergarten.* Portsmouth, NH: Heinemann.

Regalla, Lisa. 2016. "Developing a Maker Mindset." In *Makeology: Makerspaces as Learning Environments,* vol. 1, edited by Kylie Peppler, Erica Rosenfeld Halverson, and Yasmin B. Kafai, 257–72. New York: Routledge.

Resnick, Mitchel. 2016. "All I Really Need to Know (About Creative Thinking) I Learned (By Studying How Children Learn) in Kindergarten." MIT Media Lab. http://web.media.mit.edu/~mres/papers/kindergarten-learning-approach.pdf.

Ritchhart, Ron. 2015. *Creating Cultures of Thinking: The 8 Forces We Must Master to Truly Transform Our Schools.* San Francisco: Jossey-Bass.

Ritchhart, Ron, Mark Church, and Karin Morrison. 2011. *Making Thinking Visible: How to Promote Engagement, Understanding, and Independence for All Learners.* San Francisco: Jossey-Bass.

Rosenblatt, Louise. 1978. *The Reader, the Text, the Poem: The Transactional Theory of Literary Work.* Carbondale, IL: Southern University Press.

Ryan, Jennifer, Edward Clapp, Jessica Ross, and Shari Tishman. 2016. "Making, Thinking, and Understanding: A Dispositional Approach to Maker-Centered Learning." In *Makeology: Makers as Learners,* vol. 2, edited by Kylie Peppler, Erica Rosenfeld Halverson, and Yasmin B. Kafai, 29–44. New York: Routledge.

Seitz, Hilary. 2008. "The Power of Documentation in the Early Childhood Classroom." *Young Children* 2 (5): 88–93.

Stacey, Susan. 2015. *Pedagogical Documentation in Early Childhood: Sharing Children's Learning and Teachers' Thinking.* St. Paul, MN: Redleaf Press.

Swartz, Mallary. 2005. "Playdough: What's Standard about It?" *Young Children* (March): 100–09.

Trawick-Smith, Jeffrey, Jennifer Wolff, Marley Koschel, and Jamie Vallarelli. 2015. "Which Toys Promote High-Quality Play? Reflections on the Five-Year Anniversary of the TIMPANI Study." In *Spotlight on Young Children: Exploring Play,* edited by Holly Bohart, Kathy Charner, and Derry Koralek, 65–74. Washington, DC: National Association for the Education of Young Children.

Tulley, Gever. 2009. "Life Lessons through Tinkering." TED TALK. February 7. www.ted.com/talks/gever_tulley_s_tinkering_school_in_action.

Turner, Mark. 1996. *The Literary Mind: The Origins of Thought and Language.* New York: Oxford University Press.

Wardrip, Peter, and Lisa Brahms. 2014. "Mobile MAKESHOP: Preliminary Findings from Two School Sites." http://fablearn.stanford.edu/2014/wp-content/uploads/fl2014_submission_49.pdf.

———. 2015. "Learning Practices of Making: Developing a Framework for Design." Proceedings of the 14th International Conference on Interaction Design and Children, 375–78.

Wesch, Michael. 2013. TEDXkc. "Knowledgeable to Knowledge-able." Accessed May 4. www.youtube.com/watch?v=LeaAHv4UTI8.

Wilkinson, Karen, Luigi Anzivino, and Mike Petrich. 2016. "The Big Idea Is Their Idea." In *Makeology: Makers as Learners*, vol. 2, edited by Kylie Peppler, Erica Rosenfeld Halverson, and Yasmin B. Kafai, 161–80. New York: Routledge.

Wohlwend, Karen. 2008. "Play as a Literacy of Possibilities: Expanding Meanings in Practices, Materials, and Spaces." *Language Arts* 86 (2): 127–36.

———. 2013. *Literacy Playshop: New Literacies, Popular Media, and Play in the Early Childhood Classroom*. New York: Teachers College Press.

Wohlwend, Karen, Anna Keune, and Kylie Peppler. 2016. "Design Playshop: Preschoolers Making, Playing, and Learning with Squishy Circuits." In *Makeology: Makerspaces as Learning Environments*, vol. 1, edited by Kylie Peppler, Erica Rosenfeld Halverson, and Yasmin B. Kafai, 83–96. New York: Routledge.

Wurm, Julianne. 2005. *Working in the Reggio Way: A Beginner's Guide for American Teachers*. St. Paul, MN: Redleaf Press.

Resources

Below are some resources mentioned in the text that you might want a few more details about. We hope this list inspires your StoryMaking as you create engaging spaces and opportunities for your children to imagine, play, make and share with whatever topic you choose to explore. Happy StoryMaking!

To investigate adding quality materials to your makerspaces, we referenced:

- *Kodo Kids* designs products and toys for children that encourage investigation based learning and open-ended play. They now offer a new maker line of furniture. https://kodokids.com

- *Dr. Drew's Blocks* are an award-winning educational toy for young children and families. They promote creative play and serve as a tool for developing mathematical thinking, science concepts, and literacy skills. http://www.drdrewsblocks.com

- *Bristle Blocks* are soft, textured, and easy to connect to make stories. They are especially useful for children who have difficulty stacking blocks, as they stay connected more easily than wooden blocks. http://www.battatco.com/collections/bristle-blocks

- *Magna Tiles* were originally created to teach children about shapes, but they are perfect for building castles, jungles, houses, and more as children use them to make their stories. The magnetic sides make StoryMaking easy for little hands. https://www.magnatiles.com/products

- *Kapla Blocks* are based on the progressions of the uneven numbers 1:3:5. Three thicknesses for one width and five widths for one length. This ratio opens a whole new way of building and StoryMaking. http://www.kaplaus.com/about/the-history -of-kapla

To investigate Story Workshop:

The Opal School at the Portland Children's Museum wondered about the connection between literacy and the arts and developed these wonderful resources.

- This series of videos offer a view of their Story Workshop structure: https:// www.youtube.com/playlist?list=PLJVtbFRTqqS-JGHIMRo3RB7v0jQNtUB72

- The accompanying text: http://opalschoolblog.typepad.com/files/equity-and -access-through-story-workshop.pdf

- Their multimedia publication: http://www.portlandcm.org/shop/ educational-materials/story-workshop-teach-pack

Index

Page numbers in *italics* indicate figures or photos.